Goodbye,
Friend

Goodbye, Friend

Healing Wisdom for Anyone Who Has Ever Lost a Pet

REVISED EDITION

Gary Kowalski

New World Library
Novato, California

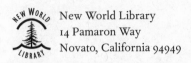

New World Library
14 Pamaron Way
Novato, California 94949

The permissions acknowledgments on pages 173–174 are an extension of the copyright page.

Text design by Tona Pearce Myers

Library of Congress Cataloging-in-Publication Data

Kowalski, Gary A.
 Goodbye, friend : healing wisdom for anyone who has ever lost a pet / Gary Kowalski. — Rev. ed.
    p.   cm.
ISBN 978-1-60868-086-3 (pbk. : alk. paper)
1. Pet owners—Psychology. 2. Pets—Death—Psychological aspects. 3. Bereavement—Psychological aspects. I. Title.
SF411.47.K68 2012
636.088'7—dc23   2011048957

Originally published in 1997 by Stillpoint Publishing
First printing of revised edition, March 2012
ISBN 978-1-60868-086-3
Printed in the USA on 100% postconsumer-waste recycled paper

New World Library is a proud member of the Green Press Initiative.

10 9 8 7 6 5 4 3 2 1

Contents

Special Section

Some have left
and others are about to leave,
so why should we be sorry
that we too must go?
And yet our hearts are sad
that on this mighty road
the friends we meet can set
no place to meet again.

— Translated from the Sanskrit by DANIEL INGALLS

1. Pets Are Not Petty

EVERYTHING DIES: goldfish, great blue whales, friends, and people we love. There is a wistful sadness that accompanies the realization that all life must eventually come to an end. Accepting death and learning to live with joy in spite of it are difficult challenges, and this is true whether we are saying farewell to a person who has been close to us or to an animal that has been part of our family circle. The grief we feel when a relationship is severed can be intense.

This is a book for all those who have ever lost a cat, a dog, or another animal companion. These creatures are commonly called *pets*, a word that is related to *petty*, meaning "small," "insignificant," or "subordinate." For centuries, animals have been regarded as the inferiors of humankind. Some advocates of animal rights argue that we should eliminate the use of the word *pet* entirely for this reason. But, of course, *pet* can also mean "favorite," "cherished," or "especially near and dear," and it is for pet lovers in this sense that this work is intended.

That includes most of us. When I was a theological student, in training for my eventual role as a clergyman, one of my professors warned the pupils in his preaching class never to mention the topic of dogs during a sermon. The reason? Listeners would immediately begin to think of all the odd canine characters they had encountered throughout the years. Whatever point the minister was making would be gone for good as the congregation drifted away in reverie and reminiscence.

There was Flush, for example, a springer spaniel named for Elizabeth Barrett Browning's more famous dog (who was the subject of a full-length biography by Virginia Woolf). My mother remembers Flush from her childhood during the Depression. In those lean times, meat was hard to come by, and the dog learned to love vegetables instead — the potato peels and carrot tops that were stewed for him — along with the fruit from the peach tree out back. His ears were so keen that he could hear the telltale plump of a peach when it plummeted in the night. He ate so many of the overripe desserts that his teeth were set on edge, and my mother vividly recalls the poor creature moaning because of his sore gums even as he gobbled down the goodies. Some brute finally poisoned him. But for my mom (who currently has no pets, nor does she even like dogs in general), the memories of Flush are still fresh, after more than sixty years.

Most of us have known a dog like that or some other animal that has charmed its way into our hearts. The tears we shed when these creatures die are genuine, for our pets have an important place in our lives. Their gentle, trusting presence becomes a dependable part of our daily routine. They share our mealtimes and befriend us as playmates. They are with us on outings and adventures, and they accompany us in moments of quiet introspection. We sense the warmth of their affection and the depth of their loyalty, forming emotional bonds that can be as strong and nurturing as any other in life. When these attachments are broken, we can experience a sense of emptiness and loss. We may feel depressed, numb, lost, or angry.

For some people, the death of a pet may represent the greatest loss they have ever encountered. Not long ago, a college professor wrote to tell me about some informal research he had conducted at the university in West Virginia where he had taught for many years. It was his custom there to begin his introductory psychology classes by asking students to write down memories of their happiest or saddest moments.

Among women, he found, the saddest events usually concerned the death of a grandparent or another close relative. For young men, rather curiously, the saddest memories typically involved the death of a dog. He says he was never able to fully probe that response to account for the gender difference. What was striking was that when asked to recall their deepest personal sorrow, so many young adults would hark back to the death of a pet.

Acknowledging loss and the feelings that go with it are an essential part of healing. Expressions of grief are the way we move through our pain toward acceptance and resolution. We need the opportunity to cry, shout, or shake our fists, if we feel like it — all healthy forms of catharsis and emotional release. It hurts, and we need to say so.

Even more, we need to have our feelings affirmed by others. Of course, no one else can fix what's wrong. There are no magic words anyone can utter that will fill the gap left when a good friend dies. Pets would be petty indeed if their loss could be so easily overcome. But while no one else can take away our grief, the care and concern of others ensures that we need not mourn alone. Knowing that others have wrestled with similar losses makes our own sorrow easier to bear.

Still, we may feel a little sheepish about sharing such a vulnerable part of ourselves. A reservation can arise — an inner doubt. Won't other people think it odd to become so distraught over a mere animal? Some might consider it laughable. The humorist Garrison Keillor, for example, once wrote a comic sketch about a judge in a poetry contest who had to read through barrelfuls of bad verse, including some fairly amateurish elegies for departed critters. But even Mr. Keillor seems to understand that losing a pet can be wrenching and that there is nothing particularly funny about it. To his credit, he has

written his own poem, "In Memory of Our Cat, Ralph."
Here is an excerpt:

When we got home, it was almost dark.
Our neighbor waited on the walk.
"I'm sorry, I have bad news," he said.
"Your cat, the gray black one, is dead.
I found him by the garage an hour ago."
"Thank you," I said, "for letting us know."

We dug a hole in the flower bed,
The lilac bushes overhead,
Where this cat loved to lie in spring
And roll in the dirt and eat the green
Delicious first spring buds,
And laid him down and covered him up,
Wrapped in a piece of tablecloth,
Our good old cat laid in the earth.

We quickly turned and went inside
The empty house and sat and cried
Softly in the dark some tears
For that familiar voice, that fur,
That soft weight missing from our laps,
That we had loved too well perhaps
And mourned from weakness of the heart:
A childish weakness, to regard
An animal whose life is brief
With such affection and such grief.

"If this is foolish," Keillor writes in the final stanza, "so be it." But it is not foolish or childish — merely human. Our sense of loss deserves to be respected, not belittled.

Fortunately, more and more counselors, clergy, and therapists are beginning to realize this. Some Humane Societies now offer grief groups for those who have lost an animal companion. For those who need a listening ear, the American Society for the Prevention of Cruelty to Animals offers a telephone hotline, as do several state veterinary schools. You can join pet-loss groups on the Internet. Some stationery companies even have special sympathy cards for the occasion.

Yet still more is needed. At last count, there were eighty-two million household cats and seventy-two million dogs in the United States, as well as an untold assortment of gerbils, rabbits, parrots, and other pets. Every year thousands of people suffer inwardly because they are without solace or support when their animals die. For those who want a healing connection, this book is one more point of contact.

Can a book help? In *Winnie the Pooh*, the author A. A. Milne describes a situation in which Pooh, after eating several jars of honey, becomes stuck in the entrance of his friend Rabbit's burrow. Although the residents of the Hundred Acre Wood push and pull, he is jammed so tightly that he cannot budge. With a sigh and a tear, the overweight bear realizes that he will have to remain in the hole, on a strict diet, until he is slim enough to come out.

He resigns himself, with one final request. "Would you read a Sustaining Book," he earnestly asks Christopher Robin, "such as would comfort a Wedged Bear in Great Tightness?"

To all those who feel stuck, whether in apathy or resentment or just down in the dumps, these pages are dedicated. Perhaps they will help you out of whatever hole you are in. And what holds true for bears may also pertain to books: fatter is not always better. For while this is a small volume, its aim and its subject — grieving and recovering after the loss of a pet — are anything but petty.

I have done mostly what most men do,
And pushed it out of my mind;
But I can't forget, if I wanted to,
Four-Feet trotting behind.

Day after day, the whole day through —
Wherever my road inclined —
Four-Feet said, "I am coming with you!"
And trotted along behind.

— RUDYARD KIPLING, "Four-Feet"

2. Four-Footed Comforters

As a parish minister, I know how hard it is to lose a beloved dog or cat. People often turn to me for comfort when their pets die. I once received a handwritten note just a few moments before our morning worship service was to begin: Would I please announce that Oatmeal, the canine companion of a woman attending our church, had passed away the previous week? Oatmeal had been an old dog, much loved by his mistress, who apparently felt the loss keenly.

Briefly, I debated with myself. I wondered how others in the congregation would react to including such an item among the joys and concerns we normally share on Sunday morning. Would they consider such an announcement out of place?

I was glad that I followed my instincts, for several weeks later I received another note thanking me for acknowledging Oatmeal's death. Simply having her sorrow recognized and validated in a religious setting proved deeply comforting to the dog's owner.

I use the term *owner* with hesitation. We may be the legal custodians of our animal companions and be responsible for their well-being, but while animals may be many things — cantankerous, humorous, neurotic, or supremely sane — they are never merely property. They are hardly in the same category as personal possessions. Many people think of pets as members of their extended family. As any animal lover can testify, they have likes and dislikes, moods, and feelings that are very much like our own.

In this connection, it is interesting to realize that we are not the only animals who grieve. Other species appear to have at least an incipient understanding of death and may experience all the pangs of separation when a loved one dies. For example, in his book *Lucy: Growing Up Human*, Maurice Temerlin tells how the chimpanzee that he and his wife had reared from infancy reacted to the discovery that her pet cat had met its end:

> I was in the courtyard at the time, and I heard a scream coming from inside Lucy's rooftop room. It was a different kind of scream from any I had ever heard, and I rushed immediately to the roof of the house. The cat was dead on the floor, of

undetermined causes. Lucy was at the other end of the room, obviously quite shaken.

The two animals had been inseparable friends, and Lucy was clearly affected. She stared at the body fixedly, tentatively raised a finger as if to touch it, but then withdrew her hand with a nervous shake without making contact.

Three months later, leafing through a copy of *Psychology Today* (her "foster father," Maurice, was a therapist), the ape came across an article on chimps that happened to include a photo of herself and the deceased kitten. For five minutes, Lucy sat immobile, then she began to gesture rapidly over and over in American Sign Language, "Lucy's cat, Lucy's cat." Sadness is apparently not a uniquely human response to death. Even a chimp can miss its companion and may go on mourning for quite some time.

Some animals appear to shed tears as we do. The Ramayana, a Hindu epic from 2500 BCE, described elephants weeping. This phenomenon was confirmed by the naturalist Charles Darwin, who related incidents of these beasts in captivity. Sorry to lose their freedom, they lay "motionless on the ground, with no other indication of suffering than the tears which suffused their eyes and flowed incessantly."

In his book *Crying: The Mystery of Tears*, Dr. William Frey reports other instances. A woman in Texas had a dog that was killed by a car. Afterward, the woman's other dog lay on the site of the grave for weeks with large tears rolling down its face. Such anecdotes are common, Frey notes, and although some experts dispute their veracity, there is little reason to doubt that whether or not they actually shed tears, other creatures do react to loss with anxiety and alarm, much as we do. In a very literal sense, therefore, it is natural for us to weep at the time of death. It may be an instinctive response to bereavement, one common to many species. For me it is comforting to know that in our struggle to come to terms with loss, we human beings are not alone.

But in our culture it is not easy to grieve or say goodbye. Especially in the case of animals, the suffering we experience may be minimized. While a death in the human community is almost always attended with some rituals of mourning, the passing of a dog or cat is seldom marked by any solemn rites. Condolences can be expected when a person dies, but in the case of a pet we are less apt to receive any expressions of sympathy or understanding. Although one's friends and family will gather for support in the event of a human death, those who grieve for a pet will most likely go home at night to a house that feels empty and abandoned. A few people may empathize, but many will not. We will probably be expected to carry on with our work and other day-to-day responsibilities as though nothing serious has happened.

Yet the loss of a friend is always cause for concern. We know, for instance, that animals can play a significant role in human health. Studies have shown that the simple act of stroking a dog or a cat, or even just holding an animal on one's lap, can slow the pulse rate and lower blood pressure. (The combination of touch and talk with an animal seems to be even more beneficial than similar contact with another human being.) People who have pets have a lower risk of heart disease and tend to live longer than people who lack such companionship. One experiment showed that even sitting quietly in front of an aquarium can have positive physiological effects, much like meditation.

Pets are good medicine. I came to a firsthand appreciation of this many years ago when I worked in a halfway house for people with mental illness. One of our residents was a young woman named Peggy. About nineteen years old, she had long brown hair and a beautiful, shy smile. She had tried to cut her wrists more times than I care to remember. Diagnosed with schizophrenia, Peggy lived in a world of her own that neither I nor the other counselors or psychiatrists who worked with her could fully enter. Her lifeline was her dog, a pure white Samoyed named Alfonse. As long as Alfonse was thriving and well cared for, we knew that Peggy was all right. Grooming, feeding, and walking the dog were the points of stability and wellness in Peggy's life. Whenever the dog was neglected, however, it was a sign that Peggy had become self-destructive and might be in danger of hurting herself. Alfonse was, in a certain sense, Peggy's alter ego: a four-legged, furry window into her otherwise hidden inner life.

Small wonder that animals have now become a standard feature in many hospitals and other therapeutic environments. Where else can we find such unconditional regard or such sweet spontaneity? Animals seem to know when we are hurting and instinctively care for us in times of need. Michael Ward, who lives in North Carolina, wrote me a letter not long ago that convinced me of this. "My girlfriend was going through a very hard time in her life," he explains.

> I tried to console her as best I could, but sometimes words are not enough. She asked to stay over that night so she wouldn't be alone at her apartment. She lay down, ready to go to sleep, and what happened next amazed me. My dog, Grish, jumped in bed, laid his massive black Lab head down on her stomach, and stayed there all night. He has never done that before or since.

Many others have had similar experiences. In one remarkable case, a boy who was comatose and who had resisted all previous efforts at resuscitation finally regained consciousness thanks to his pet dog, Rusty. The child, a victim of head injury, had been unconscious for ten days. As family members in the hospital room discussed various matters that included mention of the dog, they noticed a slight change of expression on the boy's face. After conferring with the doctors, they brought the animal to the hospital room. The boy then reawakened as Rusty began to lick his hands and his face.

In less dramatic ways as well, our pets help us through hard times. "In dark hours," the poet W. H. Auden wrote of his dog Rolfi, "your silence may be of more help than many two-legged comforters."

It can be shattering when these creatures die. We may feel as though we have lost part of ourselves. Unfortunately, there is no instant repair kit for the soul, nor is there any simple method that can be mechanically followed to restore oneself to wholeness. Each person's grieving is likely to be singular. There is something unpredictable (and yet dependable) about the process.

Grief and healing are both part of the current of life, each moving at its own ordained pace. No one can say how long we will mourn. Grieving may commonly be measured in days or weeks, but it can last for months or even longer, as happened with the vaudeville performer Bill "Bojangles" Robinson, a street dancer made famous in lyrics about his life. Speaking through tears, Bojangles explains how he danced for years at minstrel shows and carnivals across the South. After fifteen years of traveling about, his dog "up and died," the song records. Twenty years later, the singer is still grieving.

Many people report feeling choked up by the memory of a beloved pet years after the animal is gone. Some mental health professionals suppose that feelings of sadness will usually dissipate within a week or two (much of the literature labels extended grieving as "pathological"), but in many cases they underestimate the pain involved.

After more than two decades, my friend Iris still gets a catch in her voice when she talks about her horse Sentimental Journey (the title of a song that was popular when she named him as a foal). She shared the prime of her life with him, from the time she was sixteen until her middle forties. The daily contact of that twenty-nine-year relationship and the physical immediacy of it created a visceral bond, she says, that was even stronger than the one she shared with her family. "He was more of a permanent fixture in my life than parents, school, even husband and child," she notes. "How could his death not affect me?"

Iris has since owned other horses, as well as several dogs (when one shows signs of aging, she adopts another to ease the transition). She took in a calf that was rescued from the slaughterhouse — the animal finally died of heart problems, but at least it had a shot at life — and even a raccoon named Harry, which broke its neck in a fall. Caring for so many critters has meant a lot of loss. But Iris, who has been the leader of our statewide effort to ban the leghold trap — a cause she adopted when one of her own pets was mangled by one of these diabolical devices — cares passionately about animals. For her, life without this varied menagerie would be hard to imagine.

"Until one has loved an animal," wrote Anatole France, "a part of one's soul remains unawakened." Almost anyone who has ever let an animal under his or her skin will agree that for all the aggravations and heartaches that come with having a pet, the return in love, affection, and memory can make it all worthwhile.

A faithful friend is a strong protection.
A person who has found one has found a treasure.
A faithful friend is beyond price,
And his value cannot be weighed.
A faithful friend is a life-giving medicine.

— The Apocrypha

3. Kindness Begins at Home

THE DOG HAS BEEN CALLED MAN'S BEST FRIEND, but other creatures also make equally fine companions. When they are gone, we may have to work a little harder than usual to be compassionate with ourselves. We must become our own best friends.

One of the reasons we value pets is that they help to keep us grounded. Our companion animals exemplify healthy living. When I begin to worry excessively, my dog, Chinook, can pull me out of my brooding and help put my problems in proper perspective. If I become too serious, he invites me to join in frolicking and play. Because animals have wants that are few and basic, they can teach us to slow down, simplify, and concentrate on the essentials.

Particularly at a time of loss, we need to pay extra attention to taking care of our own animal needs. For instance:

- ANIMALS NEED TO EAT. So do you, even if in your grieving you seem to have little appetite.
- ANIMALS NEED TO EXERCISE. Remember that you do, too. Take a walk or go to the gym, even though you may feel listless or worn down.
- ANIMALS NEED TO SLEEP. A physical workout will help you get a good night's rest, which is often a problem for people who are upset.
- ANIMALS NEED TO HAVE FUN. If you especially enjoy certain activities, make sure to build them into your schedule.
- ANIMALS NEED COMPANIONSHIP. Try to make an extra effort to reach out to others at a time of separation, when you are likely to feel especially isolated.

Another lesson animals teach us is the importance of routine. Chinook, for instance, likes his meals at the proper intervals, with punctual trips to the park in the morning and evening hours. Unless it's an extra biscuit at bedtime, the ideal day for him holds few or no surprises.

Routines are important to people, too. For this reason, it is not usually a good idea to make any major decisions in the period immediately after a loss. Our judgment frequently suffers when we are under stress. If possible, postpone making any big changes in your life. Stick to the familiar. This is probably not the moment to replace your pet, for instance, nor is it the time to vow that you will never have another. Allow yourself time to absorb and adjust to the situation.

At the same time, when we suffer a loss, our routines will invariably be disrupted. A death means that the pattern of life has changed. Ingrained habits — going for a walk with the dog every evening, setting out food for the cat before work — will serve as persistent reminders of the loss that has befallen us. Like a person who has recently been widowed and automatically makes two cups of coffee instead of one, we may have to be retrained. Paradoxically, we may spend more time thinking about our pets after they are gone than we did while they were alive. They become noticeable by their absence.

One loss accentuates others. I think in this regard of Amy, who shared a cup of coffee with me not long ago. Amy lost her cat last fall. Mittens was quite old, but neither Amy nor her friend Chris was sure of his precise age, since fifteen years ago he had simply shown up and moved in, quite as though he owned the place. Amy and Chris were living together in an old farmhouse, and the twosome became a threesome. They went on picnics together and shared vacations. Amy and Chris even talked about getting married, but the plans were always postponed, and eventually Chris took a promotion that required him to move to another city. For Amy, at age thirty-seven, the dream of having a family now seems to be fading. Months have passed, but she still misses Mittens. The cat's death put a period on an important chapter of her life.

Each of us carries long-standing loads of disappointment and disillusion, and any loss can open old wounds. Depending on their situation, some people will be harder hit than others. Those who live alone or who have no dependents, for example, may be especially affected. One of our basic human satisfactions is the feeling of being needed, and attending to an animal gives many people a daily sense of being useful. It is important to know that you make a difference, at least to one appreciative creature. For such people, losing a pet can mean losing a sense of purpose.

For the elderly, the death of a pet can be a reminder of their own mortality. For adolescents, who may feel misunderstood by parents and estranged from other family members, a dog or a cat may be the only trusted friend in whom they can confide. For couples who are childless or whose children have left the nest, an animal will often become a surrogate son or daughter. In each case, coping with pet loss can be difficult.

Some pets may be more deeply missed than others. In a study at the University of Pennsylvania, trained bereavement counselors were paired with people who were mourning for their pets in an effort to understand more about this kind of loss. The research showed that individuals who lose a cat may have a more severe grief reaction and need greater follow-up than those who lose a dog.

It seems peculiar. Do cats, as creatures that can be

perfectly happy living in a small apartment, tend to be adopted more frequently by people who live alone and lack social networks? Or does one's relationship with a cat tend to be more nuanced and understated, leaving a greater residue of unfinished business when the animal dies? Since the reasons for the finding are unclear, we should not give the study more weight than it deserves. What is certain is that both cats and dogs, as well as other pets, have a lasting claim on our affection.

It is equally certain that any change in our personal lives or any rupture in our relationships creates stress. The resulting turmoil takes a toll on our biological and psychological defenses. The pioneering work in the study of stress was done in 1967 by Thomas Holmes and R. H. Rahe, psychologists who developed the Social Re-adjustment Scale. This index assigned various points to the major traumas and minor calamities that make up the wear and tear of existence. The higher your score, the greater the threat to your personal health and well-being.

The death of a spouse was considered to be the most grievous loss, receiving 100 points on the scale. Other losses that were rated included divorce (73 points), going to jail (63 points), bankruptcy (39 points), and changing jobs (36 points), down to traffic tickets and minor infractions of the law (11 points). For whatever reason, those who devised the Social Readjustment Scale did not think that the death of a companion animal was important enough to be measured among the other strains of normal living. Perhaps the researchers considered such a loss inconsequential — less stressful even than receiving a speeding citation. Unfortunately, many people act as though animals do not (or should not) matter.

But, of course, they do matter. When clinicians interviewed middle-aged couples who had lost a household pet, most agreed it was a painful event, less stressful than the death of an immediate family member but more stressful than the death of other relatives. One study in Great Britain discovered that 10 percent of those who had lost a pet developed symptoms severe enough to warrant a visit to the doctor. This finding is consistent with the work of Holmes and Rahe, who discovered that individuals who accumulated more than 300 points on the Social Readjustment Scale within a twelve-month period had an 80 percent likelihood of falling ill, either physically or mentally, while about half of those who scored between 150 and 299 could also expect to get sick.

Like anyone else who has suffered a blow, people whose animals have died are vulnerable. One follow-up study of individuals who were mourning the loss of a companion animal found that in the weeks immediately after the death, more than 90 percent of the owners experienced some disruption of their sleep habits or had difficulty eating — both symptoms of clinical depression. More than half became withdrawn and avoided social activities. Almost 50 percent encountered job-related difficulties, missing from one to three days of work as a result of listlessness or low energy. There is even some indication that married couples are more likely to separate or divorce after the death of a household pet. All these symptoms suggest that the loss of a pet is serious business, with the potential to adversely affect one's health, career, and other relationships.

My standard advice to anyone who is grieving is to take care of yourself. Eat right. Get plenty of rest. If possible, take some time off from work, or if you can't do that, find other opportunities for relaxation and recuperation. Be good to your body. You may be depressed when your best friend dies. You may be exhausted and on edge. You have every right to feel that way. But try to treat yourself at least as well as you would any other injured and hurting creature. Remember, the precept "Be kind to animals" applies not just to the four-legged variety. It also applies to you.

For everything there is a season,
and a time for every matter under the sun:
A time to be born and a time to die;
A time to plant, and a time to pluck up what is planted;
A time to kill and a time to heal;
A time to break down and a time to build up;
A time to weep and a time to laugh;
A time to mourn and a time to dance.
A generation comes, and a generation goes,
but the earth remains forever.

— Ecclesiastes

4. To Everything There Is a Season

With more than five hundred members in my congregation, I can count on a fair number of babies being born each year, as well a certain number of people dying. Part of my job is to conduct the memorial whenever a death occurs. Although each service is different and tailored to the circumstances, I begin many of them with the same reading. I have recited the words of Ecclesiastes so often that I can recall most of them from memory: "To everything there is a season, and a time for every purpose under heaven."

It helps me to remember that our lives proceed according to a natural rhythm. The same forces that turn the seasons and move the planets carry us in their unfolding.

Stars have their life spans, and we have ours. Even the earth, which seemed to the ancient writers of the Bible to outlast time, was young once and will ultimately grow old. It's how the world stays in balance and makes room for the new.

Each living thing has its own distinct season and duration. Among mammals, a well-known rule holds that small creatures have the briefest tenure on the earth; larger ones live longer. So a mouse or a gerbil might live a year or two, a dolphin twenty to fifty years (depending on the species), and a human being threescore and ten. As body weight increases, life expectancy also tends to go up (.28 times as fast, to be exact). If the universe were kinder, the life span of a dog or a cat might be closer to our own. As it is, loss is built into the equation. From the moment we become attached to the pets who play such an important part in our lives, we know the day will come when we have to say farewell.

Built-in limits appear to govern how long any organism can live. Among *Homo sapiens*, the maximum age that has ever been reliably documented is 122 years, and although in the past century the average life expectancy of men and women in economically developed nations has increased, no one expects the record to be pushed much higher. Human cells, when cultured in the laboratory, can divide and reproduce only a finite number of times. This means that the tissues in the body eventually lose their ability to repair and regenerate themselves. As in a car with an odometer that has turned over once too often, things just wear out.

Some pets can be exceptionally long-lived. One dog named Bluey, owned by Les Hall of Victoria, Australia, reputedly lived to the ripe old age of twenty-nine years and five months, while the record-holding cat, a female tabby in Great Britain, was said to be thirty-four years old when she finally succumbed in 1957. But few dogs or cats will live to such advanced ages, nor should they. The better part of wisdom lies in accepting nature's limits.

Time restrictions apply to all of us, two-legged and four-legged. In his book *How We Die*, physician Sherwin Nuland observes that while human death certificates must legally stipulate a specific cause of death (such as stroke, cancer, or pneumonia), many people simply die of old age. Eventually, one ailment or another is bound to overcome the fading defenses of a tired body.

Although the catalog of maladies differs for other species, the principle is the same. Heart attacks among dogs and cats are rare, for instance. Having evolved as carnivores, they can handle the cholesterol that blocks and hardens human arteries and results in cardiac arrest. Degenerative heart diseases are common, however. The heart is a pump, and like any mechanical device, it tends to break down over time. Valves start to leak, and as pumping capacity is reduced, other organs (like the kidneys and the liver) are insufficiently supplied with blood and also begin to fail, creating additional complications.

Experts estimate that from 20 to 30 percent of dogs over the age of nine exhibit some degree of congestive heart disease. But those animals that are lucky enough to escape it will eventually fall victim to other illnesses. Cancer and arthritis are common causes of death among canines. The afflictions of older cats include cancer, hyperthyroidism, kidney disease, and diabetes. But the truth is that many animals perish because they have plain run out of steam.

According to the law of entropy, one of the fundamental assertions of modern physics, everything decays. High-energy systems tend to move toward low energy. A watch that is left to itself, for instance, runs down. Without outside intervention — someone to wind it or put in a new battery — it eventually stops working. In some cases, outside interventions can prolong a life; medical science proves it. But like a watch, even if the mainspring holds and the gears don't rust, we are all running out of time.

Some think the ticking of the clock may be genetically determined. That would explain why people whose parents are long-lived tend to be chronologically gifted themselves. It would also provide a reason for a species with a differing genetic makeup to display such markedly different life expectancies. As demonstrated in the list below of the comparative life spans of companion animals, the average length of life for both common and exotic pets varies widely, depending mostly on their size:

Hamsters: 1.5–2 years
Mice: 1.5–3 years
Rats: 2.5–3.5 years
Gerbils: 3–4 years
Guinea pigs: 4–5 years
Rabbits: 5–6 years
Ferrets: 5–8 years
Hedgehogs: 6–10 years
Dogs: 11–13 years
Cats: 13–17 years
Pot-bellied pigs: 20–25 years
Horses: 20–30 years

Large mammals live longer, although exceptions occur. Most dogs are bigger than cats, but they don't typically live quite as long. And human beings live even longer than our relatively large size would indicate. Our unusual longevity is both a blessing and a burden, because it means we have more time to enjoy life but must also mourn those who pass more quickly through the world.

Of course, the quality of a life can never be measured by mere quantity. People now live longer than their grandparents did, but are they any more content? While I might or might not last as long as a humpback whale, which can easily live to be one hundred, I will probably never be as serene, benign, and tolerant as one of those mellow giants. And although twelve years — the actuarial average for river otters — seems rather short to me,

I might willingly shave a few years off my life span in return for half of their joie de vivre. What counts, after all, is not living long so much as living well.

While the life expectancy of various species may differ, all might be said to enjoy the same amount of "biological time" between birth and death. Harvard biologist Stephen Jay Gould points out that because metabolic rates differ on the same scale as size and longevity, a mouse will experience as many heartbeats during its brief lifetime as an elephant will in its more prolonged existence. A dog, a cat, a horse, and a hamster will all inhale and exhale — draw breath into the lungs and release it again — about the same number of times as one another during their markedly different life spans. Everyone gets roughly the same share: eight hundred million heartbeats, and two hundred million lungfuls.

Each species appears to experience time according to its own inner rhythm, just as animals age and grow at different rates. A dog, for example, matures on its own timetable. Although people may speak casually of one "dog year" equaling seven human years, no one-to-one comparisons can actually be made. In terms of imperfect motor skills and boundless curiosity, a six-month-old puppy resembles a child of six, while a one-year-old dog might be considered the equivalent of a teenager, having sexually matured within the space of twelve months.

The dog's pace of growth slows after two years, however. From that point on, one canine year amounts to about four of our own. By the time a dog reaches twelve, its physical condition is similar to that of a person approaching seventy — one nearing the end of his or her normal life span. But while the life of another animal might seem short to us, it is surely complete and fulfilling within its own frame of reckoning. It moves along at its own proper gait.

Life is fleeting, and any loss, whether it be the death of a person or a pet, tends to make us aware of the brevity of existence. Death prompts us to self-examination. Are we getting the most out of life? What more do we need to do, be, or accomplish in our own lifetimes to feel complete? Are there places to go, people to see, or things to do or learn before we leave the world? If so, there is no time like the present. Becoming more conscious of death can make us more conscious of life as well, inviting us to reflect on the way we will spend the limited years we have available.

Nothing lives forever, but within its allotted span, every creature — the mayfly that perishes in a day as well as the redwood that survives a thousand years — has equal opportunity to savor its moment in the sun. This is a thought that helps me to make peace with death, which almost always comes too soon, both for us and for the animals we love. "To everything there is a season, and a time for every purpose under heaven."

Hear our humble prayer, O God, for our friends, the animals. Especially for animals who are suffering; for any that are hunted or lost or deserted or frightened or hungry; for all that must be put to death. We entreat for them all thy mercy and pity. And for those who deal with them, we ask a heart of compassion, gentle and kindly words. Make us true friends of the animals and so to share the blessings of the merciful.

— ALBERT SCHWEITZER

5. When Bad Things Happen to Good Creatures

My dog, Chinook, is pretty smart, but he can be awfully dumb about cars. When he was younger, I spent hours training him to respond to commands — sit, heel, stay, and come — and he is generally good about doing as I ask. But more than once he has ambled recklessly into the street, equally oblivious to my shouts and whistles and to the oncoming traffic.

Luckily, he has always escaped serious injury. But that did not keep me from becoming agitated on such occasions. Once I saw that he was out of danger and my initial panic had passed, I was annoyed with Chinook for failing to obey and irritated with myself for allowing such a dangerous situation to arise in the first place. I can only imagine how upset I would be if he were ever hurt.

Unfortunately, thousands of animals are killed every year in accidents, usually involving an automobile. When a pet dies needlessly and painfully or simply disappears without returning, it is especially hard to accept the loss.

Premature death — whether from trauma, disease, or undetermined causes — upends the comforting advice of Ecclesiastes, for life can end abruptly and out of season. Along with traffic fatalities, parvovirus and poisoning often take the lives of juvenile dogs. Leukemia, diabetes, and FIV (or feline AIDS) are killers of younger cats. In such cases, anger, guilt, regret, and "if onlys" can cloud the horizon.

The depth of feeling present on such occasions came to light some years ago when Richard Joseph wrote a letter to the editor of his local newspaper after a speeding car hit his dog, Vicky. Addressed "To the Man Who Killed My Dog," the letter touched such a sensitive nerve that it was reprinted in papers all over the country.

"I hope you were going someplace important when you drove so fast down Cross Highway across Bayberry Lane, Tuesday night," the letter began:

Maybe we'd feel better if we could imagine that you were a doctor rushing somewhere to deliver a baby or ease somebody's pain.... But even though all we saw of you was the black shadow of your car and its jumping red taillights as you roared down the road, we know too much about you to believe it. You saw the dog, you stepped on your brakes, you felt a thump, you heard a yelp and then my wife's scream. Your reflexes are better than your heart and stronger than your courage — we know that — because you jumped on the gas again and got out of there as fast as your car could carry you.

True, the dog's owner had lost his grip on the leash for a moment as he was closing the garden gate, and in just that instant the puppy had darted into the road, where it met its end. Joseph reproached himself for his own carelessness in the matter. But it was still the driver's responsibility to stop when the accident occurred. It was hard for Joseph not to feel bitter.

Within weeks, Joseph had received hundreds of sympathy letters from people who had also lost pets and were struggling with similar emotions of frustration and incompletion: The blow is sudden and unexpected, and the culprit is often unknown. There may be no time for leavetaking. Those who had suffered similar losses knew how ragged and shaken he was feeling after the accident.

Joseph's experience taught him several things about grief and healing. Seeing his dog killed by a hit-and-run driver almost destroyed his faith in human nature. How could anyone be so callous? On the other hand, the outpouring of encouragement and support he received from countless strangers told him that a solid bedrock of decency remains in most people.

The incident also reminded Joseph of the necessity

to transform misfortune into opportunity. "Loss creates sorrow," he observed, "sorrow frequently turns bitter and becomes anger, and anger destroys not only its object but the person who harbors it." Through his letter, he was able not only to vent and release his anger but also to perhaps help millions of people become a bit more careful behind the wheel. If it caused one driver to avoid one accident, he said, he would be satisfied with the outcome.

Writing a letter can be a good way to get things off your chest. Richard Joseph, as it happened, was a literary craftsman, a travel writer by trade, and he could precisely gauge the impact of his message. Most of us are not as adept at weighing our words, and it is not usually a good idea to actually mail a letter written in the heat of passion. But just articulating our indignation can help. Write your letter and then throw it away, or tell a friend just how angry you are. Express your animosity. Pound the mattress if that helps. Honor your anger, but let it go.

Anger and aggression usually erupt when we sense that we are out of control. All of us want to shape and manage our own destiny, and death represents an absolute affront to that desire. We may feel angry at our pet ("Why did he have to run into the street instead of coming when I called?"), put out by events that appear arbitrary or irrational ("I'd like to wring that driver's neck. Why was she talking on the car phone instead of watching the road?"), or mad at God, who seems to be responsible for making a world where accidents and other bad things happen.

One woman told me that after one of her dogs died, she felt a temporary surge of hostility toward her two other animals who were left behind, as though unconsciously asking the question "Why are you still alive, while my favorite is now gone?" Only when a friend pointed out that she was not treating her remaining pets very well did she realize how resentful she was feeling and how her reaction was distancing her from companions who might have been supporting her at a time of loss.

But wherever our anger is directed, the physiology is much the same. When we feel threatened, our reflexes kick in and the autonomic nervous system, which governs the involuntary organs, takes over. The heart rate rises, breathing becomes rapid, and the muscles contract in preparation for fight-or-flight. Unfortunately, staying angry does nothing to put us back in command of the situation. Instead, we are merely reacting to events and letting them control us.

Anger is one of the predictable stages of grief. First comes a sense of shock or numbness, often followed by disbelief and denial ("This can't really be happening!"). Once the mourner has accepted the reality of the situation, the pain of separation begins. Many feelings can surface at this point, for grief is not a single emotion but the whole constellation of responses that arise in a time of loss. Rage, anxiety, helplessness, and other sensations are common.

Such suffering cannot be avoided. Often, the emotions come in waves. At unexpected moments, the bereaved person may be overcome with tears. But if the ebb and flow of emotion is given scope and not suppressed, the waves of despondency become less frequent and less acute. With enough time, the mourner picks up the pieces and begins to rebuild the structures of everyday life. Eventually he or she can use the energy from the bonds that were broken to reinvest in new relationships.

Speaking of stages is naturally descriptive rather than prescriptive. Everyone's experience is different, and all feelings are valid. But it may help to know that if you are feeling furious, that is not unusual. And if you are tired of being angry and in conflict with the world, it is equally useful to know that such discordant, tumultuous feelings need not last forever.

When bad things happen, it is normal to feel bereft, bewildered, or betrayed. You are entitled to be upset. But life also requires that we forgive and move on. As Richard Joseph discovered, if you can find a constructive outlet for your anger, not only will you feel better in the long run, but you may also help to make the world a slightly better place.

See, Lord, my coat hangs in tatters,
like homespun, old, threadbare.
All that I had of zest,
all my strength,
I have given in hard work
and kept nothing back for myself.
Now
my poor head swings
to offer up all the loneliness of my heart.
Dear God,
stiff on my thickened legs
I stand here before You:
Your unprofitable servant.
Oh! of Your goodness,
give me a gentle death.
Amen.

— CARMEN BERNOS DE GASZTOLD,
    "Prayer of the Old Horse"

6. A Good Death

ALTHOUGH DEATH IS SOMETIMES ACCIDENTAL, it is often deliberately chosen, as an act of kindness, for people as well as for animals. But even when death is welcomed, it is seldom easy for those who remain behind.

A friend of mine, for instance, recently lost her father, whose health had been declining for many years. He not only had Alzheimer's and diabetes but also suffered an assortment of other ailments that finally meant he could live only with the benefit of artificial life support. He had no real hope of recovery. The day finally came when his family decided to end the struggle and remove the machines.

Death in this case might have been experienced as

a release. The time had come to go. But it was still extremely painful for my friend to sit by her father's bedside and watch the monitors recording his blood pressure slowly fall to zero as his life slipped away. The person she was closest to was gone forever. An important part of her own history had receded into the past.

Even when death is consciously chosen, it may still come with a sense of resignation and regret. When we decide to euthanize an animal, the same mixture of feelings can be present, along with a similar array of questions: "Am I doing the right thing? Are there any realistic alternatives? What would I want if I were a sick and hurting animal and could think through the choices before me?" When our pets are in chronic discomfort, or become immobilized and can no longer enjoy the activities that once gave them pleasure, we realize that the quality of their lives is diminished.

But it may still be difficult or impossible to empathize fully or to understand how an illness is experienced from the pet's point of view. While animals clearly feel pain, do they suffer the same kind of psychological distress that humans normally associate with declining health? When do we continue treatment, and at what point does the struggle become too costly, financially or emotionally? Because these are the kinds of questions that have no precise answers, we can rely only on our own judgment, along with the advice of a veterinarian. There is ample room for self-doubt and second thoughts.

Once the decision has been made to euthanize, we can

take certain steps to minimize the anguish involved, both for ourselves and for our animals. Being present at the time of death is clearly important, for even if it is hard to watch our animals being put down, it must be still more difficult to live with the unanswered questions that arise from not knowing: "Did the end come quickly? Were the last moments tense or peaceful?"

For a few people, the thought of witnessing their animals die may be too troubling to contemplate. And in some cases, a veterinarian may ask for privacy; it can be tricky to find the vein in a small animal whose pulse hardly registers, particularly with an overanxious pet owner hovering nearby. In general, however, people can offer caring and reassurance to their pets until the final moment of life, thanks to veterinarians who have become increasingly sensitive to the emotional needs of pet owners.

Recognizing that more and more people are choosing to die at home, in familiar surroundings, rather than in the antiseptic atmosphere of a hospital, some veterinarians have now begun to make house calls to give animals the same option. This was true, for instance, when very good friends of mine put down their old dog, Ben, inviting me to be present along with the vet. Ben was a big black Lab. He and Chinook had often romped together in the park and on the beach, so it felt right to be there, sharing prayers and poetry as another friend quietly strummed a guitar. After the veterinarian was finished, the family carried Ben's body outside on a soft blanket to be buried in the backyard. What a tender farewell, and one that was intentionally crafted to create gentle remembrances. Death is not always so serene.

Last moments, be warned, can be intensely physical. Relaxing muscles in the bowels and the bladder may discharge feces or urine. Sometimes the body may just go limp, but it can also convulse, releasing gasps of air (the so-called death rattle). These are reflexive actions; the animal is no longer conscious or aware of what's happening. But for the caregiver, such scenes can be disturbing to watch and may etch themselves into unpleasant memories. Best, therefore, to be prepared, like Ben's family, making sure their dog's passing was an aesthetically guided departure, well planned and surrounded by grace.

Even if the vigil is difficult or disquieting, we probably need to be close to our companions for their sake, offering comfort and calm. Emotionally, we can assist our pets to the last moment, toward the transition of death. No one knows how much a cat or a dog really understands of what we say (more than we suspect, is my guess), but when we speak to them gently and explain very simply what lies ahead — one shot, followed by drowsiness, then relief from pain, and rest for weary bodies — they can certainly intuit the feelings behind our words.

By way of analogy: I almost always talk to my dog when I know I am going out of town. I typically tell him where I am headed, how long I will be gone, what arrangements I have made for his care, and when I will be back. Whether he comprehends all the details is unimportant if I have done my best to communicate and pass on my assurances. He seems calmed by the conversation.

Even though death represents a permanent separation rather than a temporary one, the principle still holds. We can let our animals know that they are going on a trip, to a place with no struggle and no suffering. We can tell them how much we will miss them and what a special place they will always have in our hearts. We can hug them and hold them. Through what we say and how we say it, we can express our love for them rather than our need for them, giving them permission to depart on their own timetable rather than insisting that they remain here for our sake. From our tone of voice, they may sense that a major change is in the offing, but they may also understand that we will remain with them to the end and that there is ultimately nothing to fear.

Animals often understand more of these matters than most people imagine. I came to that conclusion after talking with Dawne, a veterinary technician with a degree in zoology who has long experience working with animals. When her horse Hastings had to be euthanized, she was very intentional about the event. She invited several friends to be with her and create a circle of caring and support. (Asking others to accompany you through this difficult passage is almost always a good idea.) Once all were present, she helped the weakened animal through a final dressage, the set of equestrian maneuvers that in the days of his strength were Hastings's pride and joy. Dawne assured the horse, with her words and her actions, how much she cared for him. Afterward, the company walked to a lower pasture where the earth had already been made hollow.

It was a harmonious exit, well planned and gently administered, as unperturbed as a tide flowing out to sea. When Dawne returned to the barn after the veterinarian had done his work, the other horses there all began to whicker softly, in the same breathy tones they might use to comfort a troubled colt. Apparently they knew that their herd mate was gone and wanted to offer comfort to Dawne, as well as to one another, in whatever way they could.

Perhaps our animals can guide us as well as console us at such times. For if most organisms have an innate survival instinct that drives them to cling to life against all odds, many also seem to possess an inborn sense that tells them when the time has come to let go and bow to the inevitable. That, at least, was the experience of one of my acquaintances, who told me about her mare, Kalea.

Although the horse had enjoyed fifteen years of good health and would normally be considered only middle-aged, Kalea had developed a severe illness, apparently a case of plant poisoning, which gradually damaged her liver. She had become so emaciated and weak that she actually hesitated to lie down, knowing that she might not have the strength to stand again. For some time, she had willingly allowed the veterinarian to daily insert a naso-gastric tube delivering food and medicine. This day, uncharacteristically, Kalea refused the vet's care. Although her human caregivers could have forced the issue, they decided instead to respect Kalea's wishes.

"We both knew by now her time was near, and it

seemed that Kalea was telling us as clearly as if it were in English that she was ready now," according to my informant.

Then Kalea walked, on wobbly legs, to her hay shed, where she felt safest, to silently await the end. This time there was no hesitation about lying down. Kalea was prepared. She showed no resistance, either to the sedative or to the blue syringe of Euthanal that took her last breath. Throughout, her eyes were soft, her manner trusting and relaxed. "On the last day of her life," affirmed the horse's owner, "Kalea made the decisions." She also taught those around her a lesson in facing death with dignity and courage.

One veterinarian I know with a small-animal practice in New York says she firmly believes that most creatures know when their time is up. They are ready for their departure. That opinion is shared by Connie Howard, who directs our local Humane Society. She told me that in the middle of a subzero Vermont winter, her cat had unaccountably gone into hiding under a porch — not a location the animal ordinarily chose for a midday siesta. Connie had not even realized her pet was sick. But the cat, which had end-stage renal disease, seemed to know exactly what was happening. It was doing its best to die.

Too often, though, people are not ready to take the step that is needed to assist their pets over the threshold. Some want their animals to die "naturally," not realizing that a "natural" death can often be quite painful and prolonged. Then when nature proves too ruthless to be borne, they call people like Connie or my veterinary friend for a dose of mercy in the middle of the night.

No one can blame them. Deliberately ending another creature's life is surely one of the hardest decisions we will ever have to make. But regrettably, whether through a failure of nerve, or out of false optimism — hoping for improvement in an incurable condition — many people end up making the process of dying more protracted than it has to be.

The word *euthanasia* literally means "good death." Although death seldom comes at exactly the time or in precisely the fashion we might desire, I believe it can be more than an end to life. Death can be our friend, not our foe. In many cases, euthanasia may be an intelligent choice that provides a painless alternative to unnecessary agony. It can ensure that the last moments we share with our pets are tranquil rather than tormented. When it is a compassionate response to suffering, it can become a source of wisdom and a door for growth.

Silently licking his gold-white paw,
Oh gorgeous Celestino, for
God made lovely things, yet
Our lovely cat surpasses them all;
The gold, the iron, the waterfall,
The nut, the peach, apple, granite
Are lovely things to look at, yet,
Our lovely cat surpasses them all.

— JOHN GITTINGS (age 8), "The Cat"

7. Bless the Beasts and the Children

WHEN I WAS FIVE YEARS OLD, my father died. Although I lacked the vocabulary to express it, I was overcome with grief. I remember a lump rising in my throat when other children talked about their dads — a reminder of the incomprehensible fate that had befallen me.

I wish the grown-ups in my life had taken more time to help me understand what had happened, but in those days many believed that youngsters could be "protected" from disturbing events by building a wall of silence around them. Some offered childish explanations that raised more questions than they answered, like the one offered by my kindergarten teacher, who told me, "God needed your father in heaven more than he did on earth."

As a parent and a minister, I have come to believe that the best way to help our children cope with death is by talking about it frankly and forthrightly. That rule holds whether we are discussing the loss of a person or a pet.

Most children excel at asking questions if they think it is safe to do so, but adults can sometimes be at a loss for answers because of their own discomfort or out of a misplaced desire to shelter their offspring from harsh realities. But the best policy is to be truthful with youngsters, for if they sense their elders evading a topic, they may conclude that it is too scary or worrisome to talk about. Openness, along with gentle reassurance, can allay many of their concerns.

Listen for the "questions behind the questions" children ask. "Why did my cat die?" may be a simple request for information, in which case a brief factual answer is all that is needed. The same question may also cloak unstated issues about guilt and separation (for example, "Did I cause his death? Will I die, too?"), and these will require comfort and emotional support along with understanding. "Why did my pet die?" is unlikely to be a philosophical inquiry, however, unless the child is beyond the primary grades. Younger children are not developmentally ready for such abstract thinking. Be sure what question your child is really asking before you attempt to respond.

Whenever possible, stick to the facts. Explain that when a pet dies, it no longer sees, hears, or feels anything. It will not move again or return to life. It does not suffer or sense its surroundings. Avoid using such euphemisms as "we put the pet to sleep," which are likely to leave a child afraid of going to bed at night, confused about the difference between death and normal slumber. If you explain that the pet got sick and died, be sure to add that getting sick doesn't necessarily result in death. Otherwise, your child may fear that a cough, a cold, or other normal childhood maladies will have grave consequences. You can tell your child honestly that even though all living creatures die, it is not something that boys or girls need to worry about for a very long time.

Preschool children lack understanding of the finality, or irreversibility, of death. They are prone to magical thinking and may wonder if they are somehow responsible for the pet's demise. Slightly older youngsters (ages six to nine) tend to picture death in the form of a ghost or monster and may worry that the same frightening figure who killed their pet will get them, too. Because children inhabit a world where make-believe and reality are sometimes difficult to distinguish, it is best to handle the question of death straightforwardly and with concrete answers.

Besides being honest with children, it is important to give them opportunities to express their feelings. For some, the loss of a pet may be a minor matter, but for others it will be a major trauma. At times it may be difficult to assess how deeply your child is affected, because children typically grieve in brief episodes, with tears quickly passing into apparent indifference, then returning when the child is overtired or out of sorts. The safest assumption is that your child is upset, even when outward signs of grief are not readily apparent. Jeanette Jones, a Rutgers University psychologist whose work focuses on child development, says that children typically identify the loss of a pet as the saddest experience of their lives.

It is not unusual for children to mourn the death of "pets" their parents never even knew about: a toad that lived in a neighbor's garden, or some other wild creature with whom the youngster had formed a secret alliance. The director of religious education at our church remembers grieving for such unofficial pets as a young girl. She and her friends maintained a small cemetery in a wooded lot near their neighborhood where they buried worms, dead birds, and other once-living creatures. Although she cannot remember all the details, she can recall that the burial plots were arranged in a crescent formation and that the children pretended to hold funerals for the animals. Through this kind of playacting, youngsters can explore their own fears and fantasies about the end of life. Occasionally, such feelings may be too intense to handle and go underground, surfacing only as irritability, clinginess, or other forms of acting out, until the child is strong enough to face them.

That was the case for Elisabeth Kübler-Ross, now famous for her work on death and dying. As a young girl, she had several rabbits that were her childhood pets. She was especially close to these bunnies, because as one of a set of identical triplets, she often felt as though her parents had little time for her. In fact, the rabbits seemed to be the only ones who could consistently tell Elisabeth apart from her two sisters. Since Elisabeth fed them every day, the animals must have noticed whatever slight differences distinguished her from her siblings.

One day, her father told her to choose a rabbit to take to the butcher shop to be slaughtered, cooked, and trimmed for the family table. Six months later, when he once more grew hungry for a roast, the order was repeated, then repeated again. Finally, his appetite turned to Blackie, Elisabeth's favorite rabbit. As a last resort, she set the bunny free and begged it to run away, but the animal was so attached to her that it refused to leave. For the final time, Elisabeth carried out the cruel errand and walked back home with the meat to give to her mother. The butcher had told her what a shame it was to have killed the animal. Blackie was a female, he informed her, and in another day or two she would have delivered a whole litter of baby rabbits.

Elisabeth felt such a sense of violation that for decades she suppressed all memory of the incident. Only as an adult, after having helped hundreds of terminally ill people through the steps of denial, bargaining, anger, and acceptance, could she overcome her own denial and acknowledge the rage that had been buried for so many years. It is a testament to the resilience of the human spirit that individuals like Kübler-Ross can not only recover from such frightfulness but then go on to help and heal others as well.

Fortunately, few children will experience such devastating losses or have to endure such uncaring parents. But when a pet dies, many will face all the shock, anger, guilt, and sadness that accompany the loss of a loved one, even if they cannot fully understand death or give names to all their feelings. Because they grieve intermittently, holding feelings inside until they feel safe expressing them, children may spend many years working through a death, reexperiencing its impact at successive stages of intellectual and emotional development. One should remember that what looms large in their world may seem trivial to grown-ups, but it must be respected on its own terms.

For most children, animals evoke a sense of reverence and delight. Youngsters may only partly understand their world, but they sense and appreciate it profoundly. How differently children perceive the world became clear to me just last summer. My own two children, who were six at the time, each had a goldfish. They won the fish at the county fair by tossing Ping-Pong balls into empty fishbowls. They had insisted on spending their own money to do this, despite my parental mutterings that pets should not be parceled out as prizes on a midway. I confess that to me the fish were mostly an annoyance. By the time we had purchased nets, fish food, and the other necessary paraphernalia, these "free prizes" had cost me about twenty dollars.

True to my predictions, and in spite of our best efforts to keep the fish alive, both expired within a few days and were buried in the backyard beneath small crosses in a corner by the clothesline. What surprised me was the way both children continued to ruminate about those fish for months afterward. The journals my daughter made in school were adorned with drawings of Rosie (the pet name she bestows on all her favorite playmates), and in a short autobiographical essay that my son wrote almost a year later, the fish received far more ink than his grandparents, Sunday School, sports, or other items I thought were more significant. One evening the next spring, I found two delicate apple blossoms laid upon their graves.

For me, the fish might have been a nuisance, but for my children, they were apparently symbols for Being itself: emblems of transience and transcendence for which they had neither words nor concepts but that cast a powerful spell on their minds.

How do we understand and relate to a child's inner world of nameless worries and half-imagined possibilities? Fortunately, adults can help children cope at their own level in many ways, such as the following:

- CREATE A CEREMONY. Involve children in planning a memorial for the pet. Discuss where the animal's remains should be buried. Make an appropriate marker. Decorate the grave. Regardless of age, people need to express love and respect at the time of final parting.
- READ A STORY. Many excellent books on the subject of pet loss have been written for juveniles.

Ask your local librarian for suggestions appropriate to your child's age and circumstances.

- WRITE A CINQUAIN TO CELEBRATE THE PET'S LIFE. This is one of the simplest forms of poetry, constructed of five lines, according to the following formula by line: (1) write one noun that names or identifies your subject, (2) add two adjectives that describe the noun, (3) select three verbs that tell what the noun in the first line does; (4) think of a short phrase that sums up, and (5) repeat the word from the first line or choose a synonym for it. Here is an example:

> Sammy
> sleek, sure-footed
> stalks, pounces, misses
> there will never be another
> Sammy

- DRAW A PICTURE OR MAKE A POSTER. Invite your child to recapture the qualities he or she most appreciated about the pet. With markers and paints, a youngster can express feelings that are hard to verbalize.
- INFORM CAREGIVERS. Just as for adults, children's sorrow is easier to bear when it is known and shared. Teachers, guidance counselors, and classmates can provide sympathy to a hurting child.

- RECYCLE THE PET SUPPLIES. If the child wishes, and if such gifts are accepted, donate the pet's leash, bowl, and other equipment that's in good condition to an animal shelter. It is comforting to know that other creatures will benefit from items that were part of a cherished pet's life.

For some parents, the temptation may be strong to replace a grieving youngster's pet as soon as possible, but always remember to consult the person most closely involved before making such a decision. Pets should never be given to surprise a child who may be unprepared to form another bond. Your child can help you to determine if and when the time is right.

As always, straightforward communication is essential. You can share your uncertainties, as well as what you know or surmise about death, but honest questions deserve honest answers. Speaking to children openly and without equivocation about the end of life can help them develop trust in the mystery that surrounds us all.

When despair for the world grows in me
and I wake in the night at the least sound
in fear of what my life and my children's lives may be,
I go and lie down where the wood drake
rests in his beauty on the water, and the great heron feeds.
I come into the peace of wild things
who do not tax their lives with forethought
of grief. I come into the presence of still water.
And I feel above me the day-blind stars
waiting with their light. For a time
I rest in the grace of the world, and am free.

— WENDELL BERRY, "The Peace of Wild Things"

8. Speak to the Earth

WHEN I AM FEELING BRUISED or burdened, I often find relief in nature. Walking along the lake shore near my home, where the water is deep and quiet, can take me beneath the troubled surface of my life to a place that's calm and that restores my soul. The light on the treetops kindles my spirit when it is burning low. When I think the world has been unfair and ask resentfully, "Why me?" I find a wordless answer in the outdoors. I know I am not unique in this. It's a theme I find repeated in one of the great classics of religious literature, the biblical book of Job.

This is the story of how one man copes with misfortune. Through no fault of his own, Job is visited by a series of disasters. First, he loses his cattle and other domestic animals, next his wife and children die, and finally his own health is stolen from him. Formerly a person of wealth and stature, he becomes an object of pity and some scorn among his neighbors. Angrily, Job asks why life has treated him so badly. Where is the justice when such evil befalls an innocent man? "I would speak to the Almighty," Job exclaims, "and I desire to argue my case with God."

Onto this scene come Job's three well-meaning but rather insensitive friends. What do you say to someone who's lost his home, his livelihood, his family, who's covered with boils and sitting on an ash heap, scraping his sores with a broken pot? "I know just how you feel" doesn't seem quite right.

Although it is never easy to find words that will bring consolation to one who has suffered a loss, certain errors can be avoided. Comments that give advice ("Don't take it so hard"), discount the pain involved (in the case of a pet, "It was only an animal"), or force a false cheeriness upon the mourner ("It must be God's will" or "It's all for the best") are unlikely to be well received. Unfortunately, Job's friends make all these mistakes and more. They're of little comfort to a man who needs compassion more than criticism and who needs someone to hold him rather than scold him.

But while Job is mistreated and misunderstood by his neighbors, he continues to protest to God: "Oh, that I knew where I might find him, that I might come even to his seat! I would lay my case before him and fill my mouth with arguments." Job itemizes his complaints and demands that God give some accounting or explanation for this world, which from the human point of view often seems to be rather grossly mismanaged. And Job gets his wish! For the Almighty, the Maker of Heaven and Earth, then makes a grand appearance.

God asks Job to contemplate the marvels of the natural world: the frosty storehouses of snow and hail, the hidden sources of the wind and rain, the high vaulting courses of clouds and constellations overhead. Above all, God invites Job to consider the astonishing members of the animal kingdom: the mountain goat, the wild ass and ostrich that roam freely over their domain, the ox and stallion in their might, the crocodile and hippopotamus so fierce and heedless of danger. "Is it by your wisdom that the hawk soars, and spreads his wings toward the south?" God challenges Job. "Is it at your command that the eagle mounts up and makes his nest on high?" The closing chapters of Job contain some of the world's most evocative religious verse, stunning the reader with images of a world that is wild and free, alive with the energy of creation.

The book of Job is of special interest because it is the longest epiphany in the Bible, an epiphany being a moment when the divine is revealed in all its splendor. And God appears in these pages in an unexpected role, not as an authority figure who has all the answers, but as one who interrogates and inquires, often posing riddles that seem insoluble. "Where were you when I laid the foundation of the earth?" the Almighty challenges Job. "I will question you, and you shall declare to me."

Like Job, you may feel beset with questions in your time of loss. Is there an unseen harmony behind events that seem random and discordant? Are there lessons to be learned? Where do you find hope? The uncertainties surrounding death are universal and have no quick or easy answers, the book of Job suggests. But the "not knowing" may, paradoxically, be a gateway to knowledge. The *questions* lead to the *quest*, the search for meaning, which can itself be healing and redemptive.

Thus Job is answered, but not in the way he expected. He does not receive a redress for his grievances or a logical reply to his arguments. Instead, he is swept away by a spiritual experience, found through an encounter with the magnificence of nature. "I had heard of thee by the hearing of the ear," Job says to God in the final chapter of the book, "but now my eye sees thee." Not through rational demonstration, but rather by means of a profound perceptual shift, Job regains an appreciation for the poetry of life.

Healing may be as close as the ground beneath our feet. That, it seems to me, is one lesson to be learned from the book of Job. No one, of course, can manufacture an awareness of the sacred. But like Job, we can look upward toward the Pleiades, or Orion, or the Great Bear with her children, and perhaps gain a glimmering of the infinite. Standing by the sea, we sense forces that are vast and unsearchable, and we may even feel our own difficulties diminish by contrast. Studies have shown that when hospital patients have windows in their rooms that look out on trees and grass and birds rather than on asphalt and bricks and concrete, the patients get well sooner and require fewer medications for managing pain. The natural world holds recuperative properties that can mend our bodies as well as hearts and minds.

I was reminded of this several years ago when I gathered with a group of men and women who were training to care for the bereaved and dying as volunteers in our local hospice program. The focus of the day was spirituality, and the instructor introduced it by asking each of us to respond to the question "What makes your spirit soar?" There were about twenty people present: Quakers, Catholics, Jews, and some with no particular religious affiliation. But despite the diversity in the room, there was one thing we all had in common: everyone found renewal in nature. Gazing into the gold of a setting sun or hiking above the tree line where the vistas stretch for miles stirred something profound in all of us. Some found exaltation in other places, too: in music or in silence, in scripture or in service. But without exception, we were inspired and uplifted by the power of earth and sea and sky. As we read in the book of Job:

> Ask now the beasts, and they shall teach thee;
> And the fowls of the air, and they shall teach thee;
> Or speak to the earth, and it shall teach thee;
> And the fishes of the earth shall declare unto thee;

Who knoweth not that in all these
That the hand of God hath wrought this?
In whose hand is the soul of every living thing....

Every creature embodies a divine principle, and one of the reasons we treasure our pets is that they remind us of the miracle of life. But even when they are gone, the world remains awesome in its ability to teach and transform us.

Has life lost its melody? Take time to sit and listen to the music of a forest stream. Are you dejected? Pay attention to what the bluejay says to the mountain. If we are receptive, the beings who share our living planet can bring balm to our distress. They may not answer the question "Why?" — at least not in words. But as on eagle's wings, they can lift us above discouragement.

Warm summer sun, shine kindly here;
Warm western wind, blow softly here;
Green sod above, lie light, lie light —
Good-night, dear heart, good-night, good-night.

— ROBERT RICHARDSON (adapted by Mark Twain)

9. Rest in Peace

ALONGSIDE THE OLD-FASHIONED New England meetinghouse where our congregation worships each week is a small garden, where the ashes of our departed members lie in rest. No permanent markers are visible there. Only memories inhabit the area. No urns or other lasting containers are under the surface, either. The remains are allowed to go back to the earth. I don't mind the lack of marble headstones or granite monuments, for unlike stone, the things that make life precious, including love and companionship, are fragile and perishable. But like the flowers that adorn our garden, they can bloom again and again.

People have buried their dead like this from time immemorial. Such customs are at least as old as humankind, and perhaps even older, since other species appear to have kindred rites. Elephants are known to cover the bodies of their fallen comrades with soil and brush in much the same way that we bury our friends and family members when they die. Badgers have been reported to do the same for their mates, sometimes circling the grave with plaintive moans and whimpers. For whatever reason — to find closure, to offer dignity to the dead, or to satisfy some primordial need we ourselves only partly understand — human beings share with animals in this impulse to return the physical remnants of the departed to the ground from which they came.

Some of the oldest human burials contain the remains of other creatures. One of these, for example, took place in northern Israel, where archaeologists have discovered two skeletons that had been laid side by side: an elderly human being and a puppy just a few months old. The pair had been buried together approximately twelve thousand years ago. Touchingly, the person's hand had been carefully placed to rest upon the dog's shoulder, as though petting or protecting it.

One wonders: was the animal killed deliberately, or was this a case where dog or master had followed the other to the grave? In any event, the gesture revealed by the exhumation seemed to express the timeless connection between person and pet, a relationship that outlasts even death.

According to Valerie Porter in her book *Faithful Companions*, cemeteries for dogs were quite common among the ancient Egyptians, who idolized the animals. Given special protection by Egyptian law, dogs were frequently appointed guardians of temples and often embalmed after death. The god Anubis, who guarded the portals of the netherworld and escorted souls on their last journey, was envisioned as a dog- or jackal-headed deity, a mythic association that presumably gave his more mundane canine cousins additional appeal. But one imagines that even in a culture in which animals were revered as supernatural entities, people may have felt a down-to-earth affection for their pets. Near the Great Pyramid of Cheops, a stone slab carries the following inscription from the pharaoh to his dog, indicating the personal attention given to these animals: "The dog was guard of His Majesty. Abuwityuw was his name. His Majesty ordered that he be buried ceremonially, that he be given a coffin from the royal treasury, fine linen in great quantity, and incense."

Cats were equally valued, and there was an Egyptian cat goddess named Bast. After cats died, great efforts were made to preserve their bodies through the process of mummification. They were embalmed and placed in a coffin, then commonly buried in sections of land along the Nile reserved especially for that purpose. People who lost their pets typically shaved their eyebrows as a sign of mourning.

Archaeologists recently discovered another graveyard for dogs in the Middle East that tentatively dates back to 450 BCE. All the animals in the burial ground seem to have died of natural causes; a few showed traces of arthritis. To judge from skeletal remains the dogs were of the greyhound type, and each was buried individually with great care. Apparently these were sporting hounds, esteemed by the aristocracy. The humbler classes may well have honored their own animals with similar burials but without such enduring monuments.

It seems that the need to find a suitable resting place for our animal companions is both old and deep-seated. Burials do have a practical aspect: putting bodies in the ground disposes of them permanently and hygienically. But the practice may also spring from an intuition about the nature of grieving: soil must be turned and sod broken before new life can take root. In the modern world of North America and Europe, special cemeteries for pets have existed for more than a hundred years.

A simple backyard burial may be suitable for small animals. One girl who was particularly upset by the death of her dog — she had become hysterical and had fainted on hearing the news — reported that she was especially helped by her boyfriend, who insisted that she dig the grave herself and place the dog's body in the ground with her own hands. After filling the grave, she placed on it a stone bearing the inscription HERE LIES LOVE. It was the physical act of caring for her dog's body, a parting gesture of devotion, that enabled her to bear up under very difficult circumstances.

Handling the body oneself can reinforce the finality of death and make the loss more tangible. Still, some may prefer to employ the services of a commercial pet cemetery or look to the veterinarian, an animal hospital, or a local Humane Society to assist with a cremation. Arrangements differ, but the impulse to celebrate the continuity of life even in the presence of death remains the same. Writing of her cat's death in the *New York Times*, author Mary Cantwell speaks to this common need to ritualize our parting:

> This spring, when the ground is no longer frozen and the animal mortuary delivers the little box, I will take Calypso's ashes to the country and bury them under a beach plum bush. Our first cat is interred there, along with my older daughter's kitten. A stone cat is curled under the branches. A garden ornament that was a gift from a friend, it acts as a headstone. The burial will involve a small ritual — "Goodbye, Calypso," maybe, and a farewell toast — and if I look foolish, I don't care. Ceremony is one of the crutches I use to get through life.

But ceremony is more than a crutch. Rituals are the means we use to hallow time. They mark certain moments as being momentous rather than merely momentary in their import and significance.

It would be a mistake to assume that such rites of passage must be grim or long faced. You can be serious without being somber. A friend of mine, for example, assembled a small congregation of toy animals to attend the burial of a parakeet. Epitaphs may also be whimsical: SHE NEVER KNEW SHE WAS A CAT. Such farewells may sound frivolous, but laughter and tears are close cousins. And the purpose of a memorial is not to dwell on life's unpleasantness but to commemorate the qualities that make it glad as well as poignant.

When a pet is buried, the interment is usually performed with much less pomp and circumstance than is the case with human committals. Most people seem to like an informal leave-taking and assume an idiosyncratic approach to their final partings, but the goodbyes are no less genuine for that. In an article titled "Best Damm Dog We Ever Had," Richard Meyer and David Gradwolh contrast the San Francisco National Cemetery, a military gravesite, with the neighboring Presidio Pet Cemetery, where the animals of army personnel are interred. In the former, uniform white markers stand aligned in an orderly but rather sterile procession. In the latter, homemade headstones in cheerful disarray are decorated with folk art flourishes: living plants and artificial flowers, helium balloons and colored ribbons, weather-beaten photographs of dogs and cats along with packets of "Hearty Chews." Inscriptions have a homespun integrity, like the one for Jane, a Chinese water dragon:

> She lived a full life of 10 years. She was the greatest lizard I ever knew and will be greatly missed by Emily her owner and friends Randall,

Poncho, Nellie, Mr. Iguana, Lucy Rabbit, and the many others who knew and loved her.

Unlike those of their human counterparts, these memorials are anything but restrained. They seem playful by contrast. But while no twenty-one-gun salutes, flag-draped coffins, or brass bands marked their passing, these animals could truly be said to have been buried with full honors.

When the day finally comes for me to lay my own dog's ashes in the ground, I know I will want to sing a round of "Auld Lang Syne" and spend some time looking through my family's photo albums, where my dog's pictures will always reside along with the rest of our treasured snapshots. I know I will cry, and I may even chuckle once or twice when I recall the day he ate the drapes, but the pictures will remind me that wherever their bodies may lie — beneath plum or cherry trees, under granite markers, or scattered to the winds — our animals can rest in peace. Their memories are secure within our hearts.

Apprehend God in all things, for God is in all things.
Every single creature is full of God and is a book
    about God.
Every creature is a word of God.

— MEISTER ECKHART

10. Healing Words

I HAVE DELIVERED MANY EULOGIES in my years of ministry. One of the most difficult, and one of the most healing, was for my own grandfather. Because we were so close, I felt overwhelmed with emotion. I had to pause at several points during his memorial service before I could continue speaking. But while I was on the verge of weeping, I also felt something strangely like euphoria. I experienced a profound sense of gratitude and joy for the relationship we had shared. From that episode, I learned how transformative the spoken word can be. By giving voice to the love inside us, we bring it alive and give it power — a power that is even stronger than death.

I usually counsel those who are grieving to employ the power of words by writing a eulogy for the one they love. The term itself means "good words," for a eulogy attempts to sum up the qualities that made another person memorable and worthy of our care. In the case of an animal, a eulogy could take the form of a letter, a poem, or a memoir that reflects on the traits that made that creature most endearing or stamped it with a special personality.

Of course, words are never adequate to summarize another's life. A three-dimensional being can never be reduced to the two-dimensional surface of a written page. But in attempting to articulate what made an animal lovable and unique, we may discover subtleties that were previously unspoken or not so richly appreciated.

I have written dozens of eulogies in my time, and it is always a difficult task, but when I succeed in capturing the essence of one who has died, it is one of the most satisfying things I do in my capacity as a clergyman — hard work, but rewarding. I know my words have made a difference.

Committing one's words to paper has several virtues. Writing requires active recollection, which stirs the well of memory. At the same time it creates a lasting keepsake for the future, which along with photos, paw prints, and other mementos will only grow more valuable as the years go by. Reading the words aloud also has a purpose. It heightens their impact, and by calling on the senses (shaping the syllables on the tongue and hearing the timbre of one's own voice sound upon the ear) impresses their meaning upon the awareness.

Every eulogy has a beginning, a middle, and an end, and in this respect it resembles life itself. The process of writing forces us to focus on the main story line and look for the significant details. What were the highlights of the life that is being commemorated? What difference did this animal make in our lives? Turning experience into story form is one of the ways we make sense of our lives and give meaning to existence, and bringing our stories to conclusion can help us to find closure when we are faced with death. The living manuscript that was once a work in progress has come to a definitive end. Not only is a life over; a narrative has reached completion.

Many famous writers have penned paeans to their pets, including D. H. Lawrence ("Rex"), James Thurber ("Snapshot of a Dog"), May Sarton ("The Fur Person"), and E. B. White (whose obituary for his dog Daisy concludes, "She died sniffing life, and enjoying it"). Playwright Eugene O'Neill, in his "Last Will and Testament of an Extremely Distinguished Dog," imagined a final resting place for the Dalmatian he named Silverdene,

> where each blissful hour is a mealtime; where in long evenings there are a million fireplaces with logs forever burning, and one curls oneself up and blinks into the flames and nods and dreams, remembering the old brave days on earth, and the love of one's Master and Mistress.

Poets too have eulogized their animal companions. Lord Byron's tribute to his Newfie, Boatswain, is inscribed on a monument in England's Newstead Abbey:

Near this spot
Are deposited the Remains of one
Who possessed Beauty without Vanity,
Strength without Insolence,
Courage without Ferocity,
All the Virtues of Man without his Vices....
To mark a Friend's remains these stones arise,
I never knew but one, and here he lies.

But one need not be a bestselling author or a master stylist to create a meaningful *in memoriam*. My fellow minister the Reverend Elizabeth Tarbox wrote the following thoughtful eulogy, which expresses both the sadness and the mood of reflection that can descend when a good friend dies. I have admired her work for many years, so I clipped this piece from her church newsletter as soon as I saw it, for it shows how much life can be evoked in a few well-chosen words:

Natalie was a gold and white guinea pig, with full lips and an overstated stomach. She shared her life with us, accepted our love and care, nibbled daintily on spinach and dandelion, and swooned over the very smell of strawberries. Natalie cherished her mate, Frank, and let us stroke their babies, and forgave us when we gave the babies away.

When Natalie got sick we took her to the veterinarian and were told she would not get well again, so we made that choice which we human animals have granted ourselves and asked the doctor to put her to sleep. But Natalie didn't sleep. She lay in my lap and quivered and sighed and the life that she had so generously shared with us left her little round body and she was dead.

And I thought, how curious it is that this small animal should move me so, that this little life whose whole span had been but five years should make me wrestle with my conscience about the rights of humans to have charge over animals; how strange that this lifeless furry creature with the now still body should bring me to tears.

I had personified a guinea pig. I had granted her a place and dignity in my home. Somehow by my love I had elevated her to something more than a species of rodent. But she in turn had dignified me by accepting my care. She had brought beauty into our home, and had stirred in me emotions I am glad to have: love and the desire to nurture. She had trusted me and thereby had made me trustworthy.

It is remarkable that such a diminutive creature can summon our spirits toward such immensities. But perhaps it is true that the smaller another being is or the more dependent it is, the bigger our corresponding responsibilities become. Because they are innocent, animals can help us to become wise. To the extent that they are carefree, they may enable us to become more caring.

As a parent, I know that having children is one of the things that has helped me to become more grown-up; as a pet owner, I think that caring for an animal is one of the things that has let me become more human. The Reverend Tarbox concludes her tribute to Natalie with the following prayer, which might be spoken for every living creature:

> Great God, make us friends of the animals. Make us responsible co-inhabitants with them of this fruitful planet. In our dealings with animals, may we be generous; may we exercise our power with compassion and avoid brutality; may we never debase them; may we never use their flesh or their skins wastefully to enhance our appearance; may we respect their right to a good life in their own habitat. In our dealings with animals may we remember that all life is mysterious and precious and God-given and that we are honored and blessed by their presence among us.

Can we say Amen? Through words like these, we affirm the sanctity of life, even in the presence of death. We express our gratitude for the gift of our time on earth. As the mystical writer Meister Eckhart reminded us, if the only prayer we ever said was "Thank you," that would be enough.

Words are creative. They can motivate, chasten, consecrate, and reconcile. They not only describe reality but can change it as well. We all know that words have the ability to hurt. Why shouldn't they also have the capacity to heal and transform our world? When uttered with sincerity, our words may bring us closer to a place of wholeness and peace.

Old Blue died and he died so hard,
Shook the ground in my back yard.
Dug his grave with a silver spade,
Lowered him down with links of chain.
With every link I did call his name:
Here, Blue, you good dog you.
Here, Blue, I'm a-coming too!

— American folk song

11. Guides for the Spirit

LIFE IS FULL OF INEXPLICABLE OCCURRENCES. Although I tend to be skeptical of most phenomena that might be labeled paranormal, I know enough people who have had strange experiences (many of them involving animals) to raise questions in my mind.

There were the lions my mother heard in Sicily, for instance. It was her first trip to Europe, and she along with her two traveling companions had taken a cab straight from the airport for a late check-in at their hotel. In the morning, she complained of sleeplessness. "Did you hear the lions roaring?" she asked her friends. The growling had kept her up most of the night. The others looked mystified. Neither one had heard anything, and Martin, who had visited the city many times, knew there were no zoos or circuses in the vicinity. Then his eyebrows shot up. "Do you realize," he asked, "that we are less than a block from the old coliseum?" His implication was that the roaring came from the wild beasts that were part of the gladiatorial games hundreds of years ago. Part of me would like to think there were simpler explanations. But another part will always wonder what my mother really heard that night.

Then there was the peculiar incident involving a household pet, an orange cat named Oro, that I learned about from a correspondent living in South Carolina. The family had just moved to a new home, and Oro seemed to adapt quite well, with one rather odd exception. While she made herself perfectly at home everywhere else in the house, Oro always leaped when she had to cross the threshold between the living room and the dining room. After the family had been settled in their new residence for a few months, the previous owners came calling. In the course of the conversation, they mentioned how their old dog had loved to sleep on that particular threshold. He had died in that house, many years before. Was there a faint scent remaining in the doorway, or did the cat sense the dog's lingering presence on a more subtle level? I am sure I will never know the answer.

I have the same bemused reaction to the frequent reports of pet owners who continue to sense their animals after they have departed. As a clergyman, I work with bereaved people on a regular basis, and grief counselors are well aware that in cases of human loss, the survivors often experience "visitations" from their loved ones. One study of bereavement indicated that as many as one in six of those who lose a pet may continue to hear the animal in the house or sense its presence in other ways after its death. Stories of dogs and cats who refuse to "give up the ghost" are legion.

In *Memories*, a fine tribute to his spaniel, Chris, the author John Galsworthy relates one such inexplicable incident. It was at the dark end of December, and the author's wife was in a reflective mood, when she became aware of the dog's black body passing around the room to take his place at his old, accustomed spot under the table. It was an apparition, for the animal had died some time before. She saw the dog clearly, heard the tap-tapping of his paws and toenails scratching across the floor, and even felt his warmth brush her skirt as he sidled in front of her and pressed briefly against her with his weight. Then something broke the spell — a sound or some other distraction momentarily claimed her attention — and as her consciousness returned to the room, the dog very slowly disappeared.

Some of these occurrences might be considered hallucinations. After all, the unconscious mind can be extremely creative. A dog barking in the distance can sound just like a long-lost companion; a noisy branch scraping the side of the house can be confused for a beloved pet scratching at the door. Some people dream about their pets after they have died, and at times the images can be very vivid as well as reassuring. The animal we remember as old and sick may appear as healthy and vigorous. Part of our psyche seems to be telling us not to worry about what lies beyond this world, and there may be wisdom in such messages from the unconscious.

But not every uncanny encounter can be explained away as a projection of the subconscious. One correspondent, for example, wrote to me about a strange occurrence involving their companion Ginger, who had died some years previously. "Ginger was my husband's dog and the love of his life," explained Stephanie. Of the fourteen dogs who had shared their home during their forty-five years of marriage, Ginger was exceptional.

On that fateful day in November, Stephanie's husband experienced a fatal heart attack. Shortly after she dialed 911, the paramedics were racing into the bedroom. Stephanie sat with her son-in-law and her neighbor in the kitchen down the hall, with the two young dogs she owned at that time locked out on the patio, both in plain sight. The EMTs meanwhile went to work in the bedroom.

"While the medics tried to revive my husband," Stephanie recalled, "one yelled out three different times asking us to 'remove the dog from the bedroom.' We yelled back that there was no dog, that our dogs were outside." What pooch were the paramedics talking about? After the ambulance left to take her husband to the hospital, Stephanie says, "I realized that the dog they saw was my husband's beloved Ginger," waiting to accompany him to the other side.

How would you explain the mysterious dog in the bedroom? Is there more to the world than meets the senses? Will we someday meet again? Most religions say so, and dogs appear in a surprising number of traditions as guides and escorts to the land of the dead. For the Egyptians, the lord of the underworld was Anubis, a jackal-headed god associated with mummification who protected souls on their journey to the afterlife. For the ancient Greeks, Cerberus was a giant hound who guarded the gates to the underworld. In the Rig Veda, the oldest Hindu scriptures, the first mortal to meet Death found him accompanied by two dark dogs who hunted down souls to bring them to their heavenly abode.

Equally ancient Shang dynasty tombs in China contain dogs buried in the deepest point of the pit, animals thought to be "psychopomps" leading the dead to the land of the ancestors. Ceramic dogs, considered soul guides by the natives of Mesoamerica, have been unearthed from grave shafts in western Mexico dating back more than two thousand years. In the Christian tradition, burial effigies from the tombs of medieval churches often feature sculpted dogs — marble mastiffs, spaniels, greyhounds, and less common breeds — lying at the feet of the deceased. In her article "Man's Best Friend: Guard of the Afterlife," Ann Ashby cites the distinguished art historian Kenneth Clark, who speculates the carvings may "descend from the guardian animals or fetishes that adorn tombs in every civilization accompanying the soul on its crossing of the river of death."

Why have so many far-flung civilizations identified dogs as emissaries of the beyond? Anthropologists sometimes explain such similarities of belief and ritual as the result of cultural diffusion or sporadic contact among widely separated peoples. Or perhaps dogs recommend themselves as guides because of their uncanny homing ability. One famous pup in the 1920s, a six-month-old collie-sheepdog mix named Bobbie, found his way home to Oregon from Indiana, covering nearly 3,000 miles in just six months after getting separated from his family while on vacation. From Italy comes the story of a dog who followed his master in the service of Napoleon's army on the long march to Russia. Separated by ice floes while crossing a river, the animal returned to his master a year later, having crossed half of Europe.

Some of these accounts might be apocryphal. I'm not sure my own dog could find his way back from the end of the block, unless he knew supper was waiting. But more careful studies have been done by naturalists reintroducing species into the wild. For example, five pen-reared gray wolves in Barrow, Alaska, were relocated 175 miles from the site they knew as home. At least one of the animals crossed the tough, unknown terrain all the way back to his birthplace; others were headed in the right direction, stymied only by impassable obstacles like dams and mining excavations, when their journeys ended. In another case, tame wolves escaped from their enclosures on Isle Royale in Lake Superior and were subsequently captured, then transported 30 miles from their home. All were back at base camp the next day. Stories of startling homecomings like these exist in every time and culture, wherever dogs and other members of the canine tribe are found, kindling questions and a sense of the inexplicable.

Such navigational feats border on the supernormal, if not the extrasensory. How do dogs do it? And what better companions to accompany us on our final journey?

Perhaps the explanation for Ginger and all the other curiosities is simple. Maybe there really will be a Spirit Dog there, waiting to accompany us when we die. Answers to questions like these may be beyond our knowing, yet the stories are intriguing. And until my time is up, I will always continue to wonder.

Pass to thy Rendezvous of Light,
Pangless except for us —
Who slowly ford the Mystery
Which thou hast leaped across!

—— EMILY DICKINSON

12. The Eternal Question

A LIVING CREATURE possesses an indefinable but unmistakable presence that distinguishes it from a dead one. The contrast is noticeable even before the body has had time to grow cold. Robbie Kahn, a sociologist who teaches at the University of Vermont, told me how she personally discovered what a difference a single breath can make when she shared the last moments of her dog Sarah's life. Robbie sat on the floor next to her companion. The dog drew air into its lungs quietly, in a slightly watery tone, and the interval after each exhalation grew longer. Then the final breath left the dog's body.

The change in the room was instantaneous and almost palpable. Where there were two beings present a heartbeat earlier, now there was only one. "Later," recalled Robbie, "I would remember that moment and wonder, as I still wonder, where could she have gone so suddenly, how could she be so suddenly gone?" Does the spirit simply vanish at the instant of death or somehow take flight? People have puzzled over this mystery for thousands of years.

The question of whether animals survive death, like the conundrum of human immortality, is probably unanswerable. When Koko, a lowland gorilla who learned to converse in American Sign Language, was asked the question "Where do gorillas go when they die?," she responded to her trainer with the gestures *comfortable / hole* (the sign for a hole in the ground) / *bye* (touching fingers to lips as if blowing a kiss goodbye)." Her answer suggests that other species have given some thought to what might lie beyond this world, and it is humbling to realize that Koko's ideas about the afterlife are probably as good as yours or mine.

Yet many of us would agree that heaven, however we conceive it, would be a paltry place without the animals who keep us company and provide so many of life's lighter moments. A paradise with "No Pets Allowed" posted over the pearly gates would hardly be an attractive destination.

Various religious traditions have commented on this problem. The only writer of the Bible who directly addresses the issue is Ecclesiastes, who expresses a gentle agnosticism on this, as on so many other riddles of existence: "For the fate of humans and the fate of animals is the same; as one dies, so dies the other.... Who knows whether the human spirit goes upward and the spirit of the animals goes downward to the earth?"

What happens to people and other living beings when they die is a matter of faith, on which people may differ according to their own beliefs. My own sympathies are with the woman who, when she was asked whether she wished to be buried or cremated upon her demise, replied simply, "Surprise me!"

Many Eastern traditions hold elaborate theories of the transmigration of souls from animal to human and back again. The Jataka tales, for instance, tell of the Buddha's previous incarnations in animal form, as antelope, monkey, elephant, dog, peacock, and many other creatures. Throughout these stories, the animals act as teachers and exemplars to the human characters, as in the fable of the unselfish stag that saves the life of a king who once hunted him. "I myself was the stag," the Buddha tells his listeners. In this tradition, animals, like their human counterparts, are capable of enlightenment and liberation.

For thinkers in the West, there was originally no firm distinction between the human soul and the spirits of lesser creatures. In the Biblical creation story, it is written that God created Adam as a *nefesh chaya*, usually translated from the Hebrew as a "living soul." Seeing that Adam was lonely, according to the book of Genesis, God created the four-legged and flying inhabitants of the planet, endowing each of them also with *nefesh chaya*, or living souls, to be companions for the first human. The soul, in ancient times, was identified sometimes with the blood, sometimes with the breath, the breath making such a vital, visible difference to primitive observers (as was the case for my friend Robbie). The breath of life — the inexplicable secret separating living things from inanimate matter — appeared to reside in all beings.

In Judaism, redemption has primarily been understood in communal terms rather than as individual survival beyond the grave. But the Hebrew scriptures contain numerous indications that God's mercy extends to all living things. "Every beast of the forest is mine," saith the Lord (Psalm 50). And again, "I know all the fowls of the mountains; and the wild beasts of the field are mine" (Psalm 50). The messianic vision of shalom is of a world restored to its original unity, where lion and lamb lie down together and a little child shall lead them.

Early Christians also pictured animals sharing in paradise. In the art of the catacombs, dating from the first through the fifth centuries, Jesus was frequently depicted as a good shepherd, a lamb resting over his shoulders, on which a dove was sometimes perched, too. He often held a panpipe or a lyre, ready with a melody to charm the birds and the beasts that surrounded him — lions, wolves, serpents, tortoises, dogs, dolphins, and others — his figure entwined with flowing vegetation and symbols of the earth's seasonal fertility: corn, roses, olives, and grapes. At sites like the tomb of Cyriacus, a Christian bishop martyred in 303 CE, and in the Catacombs of Domitilla, from the previous century, Jesus was virtually indistinguishable from the Greek god Orpheus, pictured as a virile youth and draped in a flowing tunic with garlands in his hair. For the first Christians, clearly, the savior they worshipped was also Lord of the Animals.

But attitudes changed over the centuries, so that by the time the King James translation of the Bible was made in 1611, the term *nefesh chaya* from Genesis was rendered as "living soul" in reference to Adam but translated as "living creatures" when applied to other species. Christianity, in its orthodox form, came to deny that other creatures share in the hope of an afterlife, but a few theologians did raise dissenting voices. John Wesley, the founder of Methodism, who was said to have covered a quarter of a million miles on horseback spreading the gospel, was convinced that he would see his trusty steed in heaven. The popular theologian C. S. Lewis also refused to exclude other creatures from eternity, speculating somewhat fiendishly that a mosquito's experience of paradise might very well include tormenting human sinners in hell!

Among Muslims there exists a lively debate over which animals share in the rewards of Jannah, the garden of delights. Jonah's whale and Solomon's ant have generally been granted entry to the gates of bliss, and the Qur'an itself speaks of camels, horses, and trees filled with singing birds. With no single authority to define Islamic doctrine, teachings and interpretations differ.

In light of such diversity of opinion, it might be unwise to be dogmatic. Surely, life after death is one topic on which people of sincere faith and goodwill may reasonably disagree. Each can hold to the vision of heaven that brings most consolation.

One of my own favorite tales comes from India, from the religious epic called the Mahabharata. Yuhisthira, the hero of this saga, is renowned for his love of *satya* (truth) and dharma (righteousness), but his character is revealed most fully at the conclusion of the drama. Arduously, Yuhisthira and his brothers ascend the peaks of the Himalayas on their final pilgrimage. One by one, the four brothers fall aside, weighed down by their accumulated karma. But Yuhisthira, who is without sin or blemish, achieves the summit, and there the king of the gods, Indra, prepares to take the hero to heaven in a golden chariot. But there is a catch: Indra tells Yuhisthira that he must leave his dog behind, as a creature not worthy of eternity. "There is no place in Heaven for persons with dogs," the almighty Indra announces.

Yuhisthira responds, "This dog, O Lord of the Past and the Present, is exceedingly devoted to me. He should go with me. My heart is full of compassion for him," and compassion is the great teaching of the Vedas.

But you've renounced everything else, Indra reasons with him. Why not sacrifice this dog, too? The realm of bliss is waiting. But Yuhisthira won't betray his friend, even if it means forgoing heaven: "It has been said that the abandonment of one that is devoted is infinitely sinful," Yuhisthira insists, as bad as slaying a Brahman or holy man. "Hence, O great Indra, I shall not abandon this dog today from desire of my happiness." That's commitment.

At this moment of supreme self-denial, the dog morphs into a deity, who had just been testing Yuhisthira. The gates of paradise open for man and mutt alike. And the beloved canine companion, Svana ("dog" in Sanskrit), takes his place in the firmament as the luminous body we know today as Sirius, the Dog Star — the brightest in the entire night sky.

I like these old stories, even if they're myths. For what is myth but a window on a truth too radiant to be gazed upon except through the tinted glass of imagination? Such stories make the night seem a little less lonely, the stars a bit closer and more welcoming. And whatever heaven is out there, up there, or beyond the farthest constellation, it's good to think that pets are allowed.

God made all the creatures and gave them our love and our fear,
To give sign, we and they are his children, one family here.

—— ROBERT BROWNING

13. The Continuum of Life

MORTALITY NUDGES INTO OUR AWARENESS at differ-
ent points in our lives. Sometimes it strikes like a fist, and
at other times it brushes alongside with the merest touch.
It tapped me on the shoulder several years ago, about the
time my wife and I were trying to have children.

Because of a serious illness in my youth, I had to take
various medicines on a daily and ongoing basis. I was
grateful for these drugs, which literally saved my life. But
it was ironic when my physicians told me that I might
never be able to have children. Tests showed that as a side
effect of the medication, I had become almost completely
infertile.

The news created a crisis of meaning for me. What
was the point of living, I asked, if one day I would vanish

from the earth and leave no progeny? Every trace of me would disappear. Each morning I walked to a small park near our home, where I would sit and think about these questions. Usually my dog, who was just a puppy then, would come along.

As I watched him run and gambol, it occurred to me that life is a continuum. Every part is connected. The dog frisking on the grass, the swallows swooping low over the field in search of insects, the ripening blackberries — each living thing is vital to the well-being of the whole.

My own life would end someday, I realized, but the important thing was that life itself would continue. Whatever was essential would be preserved.

Chinook is older now, and so am I. At eleven, he walks more slowly because of the fatty tumors under his joints. He has also had to adjust to the two children who have been added to our household, one who is adopted and one who is not. Equally enamored with both of my children, I wonder at my earlier obsession with perpetuating my own personal strand of DNA. Having a family, I understand now, is more about sharing love than sharing genes.

Doctors are sometimes wrong, I found out. Miracles do happen. Vets can be mistaken, too, like the one who told me that my dog would not last the winter. When he said that, it was no tickle in the ribs; his prediction felt more like a jab in the solar plexus. But that was two years ago, and with the help of two aspirins a day, Chinook is still game to chase a squirrel or go wading in the lake.

But doctors and veterinarians are right in their long-term prognosis. For all of us, human and otherwise, life is a condition that is 100 percent fatal. When the blow finally falls and Chinook dies, I may stagger a bit. Intellectually I know he may not last much longer, but emotionally I will probably be completely unprepared, like most others, for the coup de grâce. For some reason, though, death no longer frightens me as it once did. It too is part of the continuum.

I am reminded of a dream I once had. In the dream, I am driving down a solitary road. Dense forest lies on either side of the highway. Suddenly, a deer emerges from the thicket and leaps into the roadway, where it stands momentarily, illuminated in the bright sunshine. Where I had thought myself alone, I now find that I am regarded by an Other, exchanging looks that combine amazement and rapt attention. Then, as quickly as it appeared, the deer disappears, bounding into the dark shade of the woods on the other side of the road.

That deer is followed by another, which also appears and disappears, and then another, which likewise materializes and vanishes. Each one evokes, for me, the same surge of delight. Time stands still as the animals, one by one, leap into sight. I seem to be praying, not with my voice, but with my entire body, whose molecules are shouting, "Yes!" and "More!" Though different individuals, all the deer contained the same marvelous essence of Otherness.

The meaning of the dream was at once apparent to

me. It was about life and death, birth and rebirth. For life disappears and reappears under diverse disguises. It reveals itself for a single flashing, startling instant before returning to the impenetrable darkness from which it came. But through all its many manifestations, there endures something worthy of our wonder and awe.

The same stream flows in everyone. My old, stiff-legged dog is not the same as the romping puppy I learned to love all those years ago, though he seems no less beautiful to me. My adopted son is not the same as my biological daughter, yet I see something of myself reflected in both of them. In each child and every creature, there is a presence that awakens what is most tender and ardent in ourselves.

It is always there, ready to be rediscovered, even when we seem to lose sight of it. Having run beyond our vision, the object of our dreams will spring back into view, going and coming within the continuum of life.

Next to the encounter of death in our own bodies, the
*   most sensible calamity*
to an honest man is the death of a friend. The comfort of
*   having a friend may*
be taken away, but not that of having had one. Shall a
*   man bury his friendship with his friend?*

—— SENECA

14. Today and Tomorrow

THE PAST CANNOT BE CHANGED and can never be re-created. Yesterday is a tale that has already been told. But today and tomorrow are still before us, waiting to be realized. They are the framework in which we have to live.

What can we do when an animal companion dies? Staying busy is not a bad idea. Volunteers are always needed at animal welfare organizations, if you seek an outlet for your energy. Donations made in the memory of a pet are always welcome, too. But no amount of money can bring back the dead, and no act of ours can alter what might have been.

The human condition is tragic in this sense: we are ephemeral, transitory beings, and there is nothing we can do about it. If we fail to realize that, the urge to stay busy can devolve from purposeful engagement to frantic activity. It takes on a compulsive quality and becomes a tactic for avoiding our own feelings of loss and fragility when what we really need is to meet them head-on. We cannot avoid the darkness or find a way around it. Instead, we must pass through the shadows to reach the light.

But if the things that we can *do* are limited, the things that we can *be* are manifold: patient, accepting, and compassionate with ourselves; sensitive to the currents of sympathy that surround us; and hopeful that even in the midst of sorrow, the future will open new possibilities for life. Inside each one of us is a center that is affirming rather than negating, expansive rather than constricting. Finding that center and holding on to it can help us live creatively even when the world around us seems chaotic and confused.

Grieving takes time, and mourning sticks to no prescribed schedule. Although it will not happen instantly or immediately, the sadness we feel from losing a pet can gradually diminish while warm and funny memories remain and grow richer in our minds. We recall good times we shared. Eventually, we can look back calmly on the years gone by — never without a tinge of sorrow, but with a powerful feeling of gratitude for a wonderful friendship. We know how blessed we have been to love and be loved, even if only for a short interlude.

But while time is required, the mere passage of hours is not enough to resolve a grief. It is also important to make time our ally, working with it rather than against it as it carries us toward new cycles of life. How can we cooperate with time, the great healer, and let it perform its task?

- For today and tomorrow, we can take care of our bodies. We can eat properly, exercise regularly, and sleep at regular intervals. We can visit a physician when needed. We can allow the strength and the life-giving force that resides in flesh, muscle, nerve, and bone to restore us to vitality.

- For today and tomorrow, we can embrace our feelings. We can ask for support from family and friends. We can practice forgiveness with ourselves and others. We can realize that in our struggle to face loss we are not alone.

- For today and tomorrow, we can accept our own unique and unrepeatable life span. We can become aware of the opportunities for enjoyment and camaraderie that each day holds. We can let go of unwanted fears and fixations. We can let the past enrich us rather than enthrall us.

- For today and tomorrow, we can pay attention to nature. We can sense our connection to a world that is dynamic and alive. We can breathe deeply and walk reverently. We can notice the beauty of clouds and clover and other living creatures. We can make friends with the earth, from which we are born and to which we ultimately return.

We can awaken to the wonders that exist above our heads and beneath our feet.

- For today and tomorrow, we can cultivate inwardness. We can take time for prayer, meditation, and thoughtful reflection. We can practice stillness. We can write and journal to bring the unspoken and inarticulate into conscious awareness. We can let ourselves become channels for the universal spirit. We can be open to the guidance of dreams and inner visions.

- For today and tomorrow, we can invoke the presence of the sacred. We can worship in church, synagogue, temple, or mosque, or within the chambers of our own being. We can receive the teachings of ancient scriptures, which speak of the Eternal within a world of change, and we can hold to the truth within ourselves. We can have faith that in spite of death and parting, all is in the hands of goodness and mercy.

- Finally, we can avoid making life more complicated than it has to be. Not long ago, when I happened to be feeling particularly glum, I shared my mood with my daughter and asked if she had any good cures for the blues. "If you're feeling sad," she suggested with grade-school simplicity, "why not do some things that you think are fun?" It was sound advice, I felt, and I pass it on to you.

Healing will happen, if we let it — perhaps not this day or the next, but eventually. What is required is to persevere, one day at a time or, as one member of my congregation says who likes to plan ahead, two days at a time. If we can manage to be just a little kinder, more mindful, and in closer touch with our own healthy center — for today and tomorrow — we can trust in life to work its magic cure.

The rugged old Norsemen spoke of death as Heimgang — *home-going.*

So the snow flowers go home when they melt and flow to the sea, and the rock-ferns, after unrolling their fronds to the light and beautifying the rocks, roll them up close again in autumn and blend with the soil. Myriads of rejoicing living creatures, daily, hourly, perhaps every moment sink into death's arms, dust to dust, spirit to spirit.

— JOHN MUIR

15. A Final Gift

A MEMBER OF MY CHURCH invited me to bring my children down to her farm this spring to see the baby lambs. We set out on a sunny Sunday afternoon near the end of March and had only a short drive on unpaved roads to reach her home, with beautiful views of the neighboring hills. In Vermont, you are never far from the countryside.

There were seventeen lambs, and three of the ewes were still pregnant. A shaggy ram with massive curling horns was tethered safely in the yard, regarding us with a proprietary stare from his great yellow eyes as we entered the animals' enclosure.

None of the lambs were more than three weeks old, but all were exuberant: climbing up the small mountains of hay that had been placed there to nourish them, sliding down or being shoved aside by their brothers and sisters, then bounding once again toward the summit in an apparent effort to defy the laws of gravity. Their capers were contagious and made the children skip. Although there was still a foot of snow on the ground and we were soon heading indoors to get warm, the season of rebirth had clearly arrived.

One of the lambs was named Hope. The little creature had been delivered strong and healthy shortly after another, less fortunate, had arrived stillborn. Although such casualties are sad, they are part of the landscape for country people, who understand that death is a part of life, as much as gestation, growth, and aging. It is only in modern, technological societies that death appears as a stranger, fearsome because it is so unfamiliar in our controlled and humanly contrived environment.

For many of us who live in cities and suburbs, a family pet may be our closest living link to the cycles of nature. We may no longer be able to see lambing in the spring, and we may have to strain to hear the chorus of geese flying south in the fall, but through the creatures who share our homes, we can still experience some of the wonderment of living. Our animal companions remain part of a natural order where beginnings and endings are woven inextricably into a single garment of creation.

Whether we are seeing a kitten opening its eyes for the very first time or watching the last breath slowly leaving the frame of an old and trusted dog, we are witnessing two sides of the same marvelous event. From out of the infinite realm of possibility, a never-to-be-repeated creature comes into being, looks out briefly on the universe, passes its life force along to coming generations, then rejoins the undifferentiated vastness from which it emerged. For millions of years, this has been the pattern of life as it perpetuates itself and evolves.

Birth and Death — could any of us invent a more beautiful way to enter this world or devise a more natural route for leaving it at the end? Animals enrich our lives in countless ways, with their playfulness, their tranquility, their constancy, and their love. If they can help us remember that death is not our enemy but simply one more moment in the world's endless process of becoming, dissolution, and renewal, they will have imparted a final gift.

Special Section

A selection of readings on life and death, with re-sources for commemorating the lives of our animal companions.

Creating Your Own Ceremony

WHEN A MEMBER of my congregation dies, I usually offer the surviving members of the family a book of readings: poems, prayers, and meditations that can help them to reflect quietly on life's final episode. It helps them to gather their thoughts. It invites them to look inward at a time when the outer world may feel unmanageable or overwhelming. It connects them with a spiritual heritage in which loss is an inevitable feature of human experience but in which love is also real and abiding.

The following readings are especially intended for those who have lost a pet. The authors included here span many centuries, from ancient Rome to modern America. They represent a range of religious perspectives, from Navajo to Hindu to Christian. Some of the readings are tributes to departed companions. Others speak to the role that animals play in our lives or to the universals of resignation and hope. Because they are so varied, you will undoubtedly find some more significant than others. But it inspires confidence to know that people in every time and place have faced death and, out of their different traditions, have found reasons to trust in life.

You may wish to incorporate readings that seem especially appropriate into a service of commemoration for your pet. Such a celebration might be held at home, at the grave site, or in a park where the ashes are to be scattered. If an animal's remains are unavailable for an interment, or if you want to keep them, you might consider planting a tree or some flowers in a quiet corner, to symbolize our connection with the earth, which is the source of life and rebirth. Some people place a marker outdoors in memory of their companions or buy a special frame for their favorite photograph to hang indoors. An example of one family's ritual of leave-taking that might be used as a model in creating your own ceremony can be found at the conclusion of this section.

A memorial can be solitary, or friends and family members may be gathered in farewell. In some cases, not everyone who actually cared for a pet can be present when the animal dies. Children who grew up with the animal may be away at college, for instance. Coming to terms with the death may be especially difficult for those who lack the chance to say a personal goodbye. A memorial that is held at a later time, when all who are affected by the loss are reassembled, can offer everyone concerned an opportunity to grieve and support one another in healing.

Most memorials I conduct include a period of silence, permitting participants to be alone with their thoughts, as well as a brief time for sharing, when those present are invited to recall their best and most loving memories. If you would like to offer a eulogy, this is the time. A reading at the beginning of the service and a prayer at the end can open and close such simple ceremonies, invoking a sense of reverence and gratitude and setting apart these few minutes of affectionate tribute as sacred time. You will find words here for both ingathering and benediction. A typical ceremony might include the following elements:

- CENTERING OURSELVES. Begin with a meditation that helps you to connect with the source of your own being. Some might choose a passage from Saint Francis, while others may select one from the Bhagavad Gita or from another spiritual tradition represented here. Turn to whatever truth you find life-giving and dependable. Whether you name the object of your faith God, the Great Spirit, or Mother Earth, this reality provides the context in which all creatures live and breathe and holds out the promise of renewal.
- ACKNOWLEDGING OUR LOSS. Give expression to the sorrow that accompanies the death of a

beloved companion. Name your pain. Several readings included here convey the mood of bleakness and desolation that grief can bring. A ceremony of remembrance should be an occasion when we have permission to weep and vent our sadness.

- HONORING OUR MEMORIES. While a memorial service offers a chance to mourn, it should also offer the opportunity to give thanks. Remember everything that was outstanding, praiseworthy, or just plain peculiar about your pet. Poems like the youthful verse that John Gittings wrote for his cat Celestino, which appears at the beginning of chapter 7, or prayers like George Appleton's, which you will find in this section, celebrate the beauty we find in other creatures. Use a poem or a prayer from this book or write one of your own that gives voice to your feelings of thanksgiving.

- EXPRESSING OUR HOPE. Most memorials I conduct end with an affirmation of the life ahead. Ideally, the experience of loss inspires us to care for one another and to value each day we are given, to be kinder with ourselves and more appreciative of the world around us. You may also want to share your hopes for the future. How will you be changed as a result of the time you shared with your animal companion? In what ways would you like to live differently, or more intentionally, in years to come?

In addition to planning a memorial, you may also want to remember your pet at regular intervals after the animal's death. If your companion was ten years old, for example, you might light a candle at the dinner table for ten days following the loss. You could choose one of the readings included here to accompany such a ritual. Take a moment to recollect where you were and what you were doing during each of the years you spent together. Setting aside a prescribed period for grieving — a few minutes every morning or evening for a week or two immediately after the death — will ensure that you have at least a portion of each day reserved for time you need to mourn. Observing anniversaries, after a month has passed or yearly on the date of your animal's death, is also important for many people.

Making meaning out of life, including life's finale, is the way to transform grief into wisdom. Finding a purpose for existence is what keeps our suffering from being pointless. Moving beyond brokenness means integrating loss into a wider framework of understanding that can embrace both birth and death as parts of a larger whole. Meaning, purpose, and understanding can be discovered only within ourselves. Fortunately, the poets and philosophers of many ages and cultures are ready to aid us in our quest.

A Selection of Readings and Poems

Thou hast made the moon to measure the year
and taught the sun where to set.
When thou makest darkness and it is night,
all the beasts of the forest come forth....
All of them look expectantly to thee
to give them their food at the proper time;
what thou givest them they gather up;
when thou openest thy hand, they eat their fill.
Then thou hidest thy face, and they are restless and
    troubled;
when thou takest away their breath, they fail
and they return to the dust from which they came;
but when thou breathest into them, they recover;
thou givest new life to the earth.

— Psalm 104

Be praised, my Lord, for all your creatures.
In the first place for the blessed Brother Sun,
Who gives us the day and enlightens us through you.
Be praised, my Lord, for Sister Moon and the stars
Formed by you so bright, precious and beautiful.
Be praised, my Lord, for Brother Wind
And the airy skies, so cloudy and serene....
Be praised, my Lord, for our sister, Mother Earth,
Who nourishes us and watches us
While bringing forth abundance of fruits with colored
   flowers
And herbs....
Be praised, my Lord, for our sister, Bodily Death,
Who no living man can escape.
Praise and bless my Lord.
Render thanks.
Serve God with great humility.

—— SAINT FRANCIS OF ASSISI

∾⤙

I am that living and fiery Essence of the divine substance
that glows in the beauty of the fields. I shine in the water,
I burn in the sun, and the moon, and the stars. Mine is
the mysterious force of the invisible wind. I permeate all
things, that they may not die. I am Life.

—— HILDEGARD OF BINGEN

∾⤙

I am the self abiding
in the heart of all creatures;
I am their beginning,
their middle and their end.
Know that my brilliance,
flaming in the sun,
in the moon, and in fire,
illumines this whole universe.

— Bhagavad Gita

❧

There is not a beast on earth, nor fowl that flieth on two
wings, but they are a people like unto you, and to God
they shall return.

— The Qur'an (Surah 6, Al. An'am, or The Cattle)

❧

Know, first, that heaven, and earth's compacted frame,
And flowing waters, and the starry frame,
And both the radiant lights, one common soul
Inspires and feeds — and animates the whole.
This active mind, infused through all space,
Unites and mingles with the mighty mass:
Hence, men and beasts the breath of life obtain,
And birds of air, and monsters of the main.
Th'ethereal vigour is in all the same,
And every soul is filled with equal flame.

— VIRGIL, *The Aeneid*, translated by John Dryden

All things bright and beautiful,
All creatures great and small,
All things wise and wonderful,
The Lord God made them all.

—— CECIL FRANCES ALEXANDER

O God, we thank thee
for all the creatures thou hast made,
so perfect in their kind
great animals like the elephant and the rhinoceros,
humorous animals like the camel and the monkey,
friendly ones like the dog and the cat,
working ones like the horse and the ox,
timid ones like the squirrel and the rabbit,
majestic ones like the lion and the tiger,
for birds with their songs.
O God, give us such love for thy creation,
that love may cast out fear,
and all thy creatures and thy creation
see in men and women like us
their priest and their friend....

—— GEORGE APPLETON

The insect in the plant, the moth which spends its brief
hours of existence hovering about the candle's flame ——
nay, the life which inhabits a drop of water, is as much an

object of God's special providence as the mightiest monarch on his throne.

— HENRY BERGH, founder, American Society
for the Prevention of Cruelty to Animals

❧

We need another and wiser and perhaps more mystical concept of animals. We patronize them for their incompleteness, for their tragic fate of having taken form so far below ourselves. And therein we err, and greatly err. For the animal shall not be measured by man. In a world older and more complete than ours they move finished and complete, gifted with extensions of the senses we have lost or never attained, living by voices we shall never hear. They are not brethren; they are not underlings; they are other nations, caught with ourselves in the net of life and time, fellow prisoners of the splendour and the travail ahead.

— HENRY BESTON

❧

We should understand well that all things are the work of the Great Spirit. We should know the Great Spirit is within all things: the trees, the grasses, the rivers, the mountains, and the four-legged and winged peoples; and even more important, we should understand that the Great Spirit is also above all these things and peoples. When we do understand all this deeply in our hearts,

then we will fear, and love, and know the Great Spirit,
and then we will be and act and live as the Spirit intends.

— BLACK ELK

❧

Love all God's creation, the whole universe, and each
grain of sand. Love every leaflet, every ray of God's
light; love the beasts, love the plants, love every creature.
When you love every creature, you will understand the
mystery of God in created things.

— FYODOR DOSTOYEVSKY

❧

If I were alone in a desert and feeling afraid,
I would want a child to be with me.
For then my fear would disappear and I would be made
    strong.
This is what life in itself can do because it is so noble,
so full of pleasure and so powerful.
But if I could not have a child with me
I would like to have at least a living animal at my side to
    comfort me.
Therefore, let those who bring about wonderful things
in their big, dark books
take an animal to help them.
The life within the animal will give them strength in
    turn.
For equality gives strength, in all things and at all times.

— MEISTER ECKHART

"I don't want reassurance from you — just the truth. I know you are very young, but please tell me — what are your beliefs? Will my animals go with me?"

She stared intently into my eyes. I shifted in my chair and swallowed once or twice.

"Mrs. Stubbs, I'm afraid I'm a bit foggy about all this," I said. "But I'm absolutely certain of one thing. Wherever you are going, they are going too."

She still stared at me but her face was calm again. "Thank you, Mr. Herriot. I know you are being honest with me. That is what you really believe, isn't it?"

"I do believe it," I said. "With all my heart I believe it."

— JAMES HERRIOT, "Early Days In Darrowby"

Christopher Hogwood, Lilla said to me shortly after he died, "was a big Buddha master for us. He taught us how to love. How to love what life gives you — to love your slops. What a soul!" she said. "He was a being of pure love."

It's true. He loved company. He loved good food. He loved the warm summer sun, the belly rubs from caressing little hands. He loved this life. "That love," Lilla promised me, "is not lost. It can never be lost."

Christopher Hogwood knew how to relish the juicy savor of this fragrant, abundant, sweet, green world. To show us this would have been gift enough. But he showed us another truth as well. That a pig did not become bacon but lived fourteen years, pampered and adored till the day he died peacefully in his sleep — that's proof that we need not "be practical" all the time. We need not accept the rules that our society or species, family or fate seem to have written for us. We can choose a new way. We have the power to transform a story of sorrow into a story of healing. We can choose life over death. We can let love lead us home.

At the moment, the Pig Palace stands empty. People ask, "Will you get another pig?" This I don't know. But one thing I know for sure: a great soul can appear among us at any time, in the form of any creature. I'm keeping my eyes open.

— SY MONTGOMERY, *The Good Good Pig*

❧

Time is too slow for those who wait; too swift
For those who fear; too long for those who grieve;
Too short for those who rejoice. But for those
Who live, Time is Eternity. Hours fly, flowers
Die, new days, new ways pass by. Love stays.

— ANONYMOUS, inscription on a sundial,
   University of Virginia

❧

All things pass, all things return; eternity turns the wheel of Being. All things die, all things blossom again, eternal is the year of Being. All things break, all things are joined anew; eternally the house of Being builds itself the same. All things part, all things welcome each other again; eternally the ring of Being abides by itself. In each Now, Being begins; round each Here turns the sphere of There. The center is everywhere. Bent is the path of eternity.

— FRIEDRICH NIETZSCHE, *Thus Spake Zarathustra*

A dog's life is forlorn, dear God,
Though we may leap and sport;
Our sorrow — and it breaks our hearts —
Is that our lives are short.

"A dog's best friend is man," they say,
"Or woman — saint or knave."
So dogs long to escort those lives
From childhood to the grave.

We live too fast! At three months old
We match a child of four.
At one, we're grown-up as our friend
Who is sixteen or more.

In just two years we're as mature
As humans twenty-five.
And when we're ten, we're getting old
And lucky to survive.

Please hear our prayer, forgive our need
To leap and bark and snort,
For we must cram a world of love
Into a life so short!

— WILLIAM CLEARY, "The Doggie's Dirge"

❧

One night a man was crying,
"Allah, Allah!"
His lips grew sweet with the praising,
until a cynic said,
"So! I have heard you
calling out, but have you ever
gotten any response?"
The man had no answer for that.
He quit praying and fell into a confused sleep.
He dreamed he saw Khidr, the guide of souls,
in a thick, green foliage.
"Why did you stop praising?"
"Because I've never heard anything back."
"This longing you express
is the return message."
The grief you cry out from
draws you toward union.
Your pure sadness that wants help
is the secret cup.
Listen to the moan of a dog for its master.
That whining is the connection.

There are love dogs no one knows the names of.
Give your life to be one of them.

— JALAL AD-DIN RUMI, "Love Dogs"

❧

There is sorrow enough in the natural way
From men and women to fill our day;
And when we are certain of sorrow in store,
Why do we always arrange for more?
Brothers and Sisters, I bid you beware
Of giving your heart to a dog to tear.

When the body that lived at your single will,
With its whimper of welcome, is stilled (how still!),
When the spirit that answered your every mood
Is gone — wherever it goes — for good,
You will discover how much you care,
And will give your heart to a dog to tear.

— RUDYARD KIPLING, "The Power of the Dog"

❧

For I will consider my Cat Jeoffry.
For he is the servant of the Living God, duly and daily
    serving him.
For at the first glance of the glory of God in the East he
    worships in his way.

For this is done by wreathing his body seven times
round with elegant quickness.

For then he leaps up to catch the musk, which is the
blessing of God upon his prayer.

For he rolls upon prank to work it in.

For having done duty and received blessing he begins to
consider himself.

For this he performs in ten degrees.

For first he looks upon his fore-paws to see if they are
clean.

For secondly he kicks up behind to clear away there.

For thirdly he works it upon stretch with the fore-paws
extended.

For fourthly he sharpens his paws by wood.

For fifthly he washes himself.

For sixthly he rolls upon wash.

For seventhly, he fleas himself, that he may not be inter-
rupted upon the beat.

For eighthly he rubs himself against a post.

For ninthly he looks up for his instructions.

For tenthly he goes in quest of food.

For having consider'd God and himself he will consider
his Neighbor...

For God has blessed him in the variety of his
movements.

For, tho' he cannot fly, he is an excellent clamberer.

For his motions upon the face of the earth are more than
any other quadrupede.

For he can tread to all the measures upon the musick.

For he can swim for life.
For he can creep.

— CHRISTOPHER SMART, "Of Jeoffry, His Cat"

❧

Yes thou mayst eat thy bread, and lick the hand
That feeds thee; thou mayst frolic on the floor
At evening, and at night retire secure
To thy straw couch, and slumber unalarm'd;
For I have gain'd thy confidence, have pledged
All that is human in me, to protect
Thine unsuspecting gratitude and love.
If I survive thee, I will dig thy grave;
And, when I place thee in it, sighing say,
I knew at least one hare that had a friend.

— WILLIAM COWPER, "My Pet Hare"

❧

Do not stand at my grave and weep.
I am not there, I do not sleep.
I am a thousand winds that blow.
I am the diamond glint on snow.
I am the sunlight on ripened grain.
I am the gentle autumn rain.
When you wake in the morning hush,
I am the swift, uplifting rush
Of quiet birds in circling flight.
I am the soft starlight at night.

Do not stand at my grave and weep.
I am not there. I do not sleep.

— ANONYMOUS

❧

Nothing is ever really lost, or can be lost,
No birth, identity, form — no object of the world,
Nor life, nor force, nor any visible thing;
Appearance must not foil, nor shifted sphere confuse thy
     brain.
Ample are time and space — ample the fields of Nature.

— WALT WHITMAN, "Leaves of Grass"

❧

What is life? It is the flash of a firefly in the night. It is
the breath of a buffalo in the winter time. It is the little
shadow which runs across the grass and loses itself in the
sunset.

— CROWFOOT, chief of the Blackfeet Nation

❧

For those, O Lord, the humble beasts,
that bear with us the burden and heat of the day,
and offer their guileless lives
for the well-being of humankind;
and for the wild creatures,
whom you made wise, strong and beautiful,

we supplicate for them
Your great tenderness of heart,
for You have promised to save
both human and beast,
and great is Your loving kindness,
O Master, Savior of the world.

— ST. BASIL THE GREAT, Bishop of Caesarea

In the house of long life
I will wander.
In the house of happiness
I will wander.
With beauty before me
I will wander.
With beauty behind me
I will wander.
With beauty above me
I will wander.
With beauty below me
I will wander.
In old age traveling
On the trail of beauty
I will wander.
It shall be finished in beauty.

— Night Chant of the Navajo

Blessed are the playful, for they shall be surrounded by
    love and laughter.
Blessed are those without worry, for through them, we
    shall know peace.
Blessed are those with no possessions, for they shall be
    rich in spiritual things.
Blessed are the innocent, for theirs is the realm of
    heaven.
Blessed are the animals, and blessed are we.

—— GARY KOWALSKI

One Family's Ritual
of Leave-Taking

Remembering Lady
Loving companion, wise teacher — and forever the playful
*   retriever!*

— ERROL G. SOWERS

WHEN THE VET TOLD US our beloved twelve-year-old golden retriever had less than two months to live, we were not exactly surprised. The tumor in the middle of her back was quickly metastasizing and growing bigger every day. This condition, combined with severe arthritis in Lady's rear legs, did not portend good news. Still, her now imminent death pained our hearts.

The next six weeks were filled with both joy and sadness. Lady too somehow knew that every day was to be savored. So despite her increasing discomfort, she pushed us to play her favorite game — retrieving thrown rocks. And each time we played, the vitality of youth seemed to return, if only for a few moments.

Days before the tumor was ready to erupt through

the skin, the vet arrived at our home, medical bag in hand. We had decided to make Lady's last few hours a time of honoring her life and being fully present during her transition. Little did we know that this gift would contribute most to our own healing.

Although we didn't plan a formal ceremony, my wife, Meredith, our son, Mark, and two close friends, Jeremy and Helena, gathered with me on a sunny hillside less than fifty feet from the open grave we had dug earlier. Together we created a memorial service that embraced the following four elements:

1. HONORING THE LIFE LIVED. As we sat on the ground, I held Lady so her head rested gently in my lap. With everyone taking turns stroking her, we reminisced about the times we shared with her. With tears flowing freely down my cheeks, I recalled Lady's frequent nuzzling of my hand and the little four-footed dance she always did with a few barks thrown in whenever she wanted to play her retrieval game. Meredith recalled the proud way that Lady took a territorial stand accompanied by constant barking every time a strange dog so much as dared venture onto our property. Even the stories about her occasional digging in our flower gardens brought back fond memories.

2. GIVING REASSURANCE. We had no doubt that Lady knew her time in this physical world was drawing to a close. She gave me one long last

look with those soft brown eyes, as if to say, "It's okay. I'm ready. I'm not afraid. And thanks for being with me before I go back home." In seeking to reassure her, we found ourselves being the ones reassured. Being present when euthanasia is chosen by an animal's caretaker is absolutely an act of kindness as well as balm for lessening one's own grief and suffering.

3. RELEASING TO THE ONENESS OF LIFE. As Mark and I carried her quiet limp body and placed it lovingly into the earth, we felt a gentle lifting of our spirits, as though God were more present than usual. The energy in the air was palpable, and we knew deep inside that all would be well. In those few moments of committing a loved one's body back to Mother Earth, we realized how precious life really is and that we are all inextricably connected to one another and to the Creator.

4. REMEMBERING WITH LOVE. Our animal friends are great teachers. They participate easily in the flow of life and surely accept death with greater courage than most humans do. As we reflected on this experience of life, death, — and, we believe, rebirth — we felt richly blessed and filled with a deep sense of community. Lady's spirit was tangibly present. It was as though we would feel her laughing again, freed from a worn-out body and forever the playful retriever.

Bibliography

Abercrombie, Barbara, ed. *Cherished: 21 Writers on Animals They Have Loved and Lost*. Novato, CA: New World Library, 2011.

Ashby, Ann. "Man's Best Friend: Guard of the Afterlife." *Dog World*, July 1993.

Auden, W. H. "Talking to Dogs." *Harper's*, March 1971.

Bly, Robert. *News of the Universe: Poems of Twofold Consciousness*. San Francisco: Sierra Club Books, 1980.

Butler, Carolyn, Suzanne Hetts, and Laurel Lagoni. *Friends for Life: Loving and Losing Your Animal Companion*. Boulder, CO: Sounds True Audio, 1996.

Cantwell, Mary. "The Soul Knows No Species, nor Does Love." *New York Times*, March 22, 1990.

Clinebell, Howard. *Basic Types of Pastoral Care and Counseling*. Nashville, TN: Abingdon Press, 1984.

Frey, William. *Crying: The Mystery of Tears*. Minneapolis, MN: Winston Press, 1985.

Galsworthy, John. *Memories*. New York: Charles Scribner's Sons, 1914.

Goodman, Jacki. *The Fireside Book of Dog Stories*. New York: Simon and Schuster, 1943.

Gould, Stephen Jay. "Our Allotted Lifetimes." *Natural History* 86, no. 7 (1977).

Grollman, Earl. *Talking about Death: A Dialogue between Parent and Child*. Boston: Beacon Press, 1976.

Holmes, Thomas, and R. H. Rahe. "The Social Adjustment Rating Scale." *Journal of Psychosomatic Research* 2, (1967): 213–218.

Joseph, Richard. *A Letter to the Man Who Killed My Dog*. New York: Frederick Fell, 1956.

Kahn, Robbie Pfeufer. "Though It's Your Heart's Passion: Healing from the Death of a Family Dog." Paper presented at the American Sociological Association's Sociology of Emotions Conference, New York, August 1996.

Katcher, Aaron, ed. *New Perspectives on Our Lives with Companion Animals*. Philadelphia: University of Pennsylvania Press, 1983.

Katcher, Aaron, and Alan Beck. "Health and Caring for Living Things." *Anthrozoos* 1, no. 3 (1987): 175–183.

Keillor, Garrison. "The Poetry Judge." *Atlantic Monthly*, February 1996.

Keillor, Garrison. *We Are Still Married: Stories and Letters*. New York: Penguin Books, 1990.

Kenworthy, Jack. *Dog Training Guide*. London: Pet Library, 1969.

Kipling, Rudyard. *Collected Dog Stories*. Garden City, NY: Doubleday, Doran & Co., 1934.

Kübler-Ross, Elisabeth. *Death Is of Vital Importance*. Barrytown, NY: Station Hill Press, 1995.

Kutner, L. "For Children, the Death of a Pet Isn't Practice for Something More Serious; It's the Real Thing." *New York Times*, August 2, 1990.

Lee, Laura. "Coping with Pet Loss." *Dogs Today*, September 1996.

Levinson, Boris. "Human Grief on the Loss of an Animal Companion." *Archives of the Foundation of Thanatology* 9, no. 2 (1981): 5.

Lewis, Richard, ed. *Miracles: Poems by Children of the English-Speaking World*. New York: Simon and Schuster, 1966.

Mason, Jim. *An Unnatural Order*. New York: Continuum, 1997.

Matthews, Peter, ed. *The Guiness Book of Records*. New York: Bantam Books, 1995.

McKeown, Donal, and Earl Strimple. *Your Pet's Health from A to Z*. New York: Robert B. Luce, 1973.

Meyer, Richard E., and David M. Gradwolh. "Best Damm Dog We Ever Had: Some Folkloristic and Anthropological Observations on San Francisco's Presidio Pet Cemetery." *Journal of the Association for Gravestone Studies* 12 (1995): 206–219.

Nieburg, Herbert, and Arlene Fischer. *Pet Loss: A Thoughtful Guide for Adults and Children*. New York: Harper & Row, 1982.

Nuland, Sherwin. *How We Die: Reflections on Life's Final Chapter*. New York: Alfred A. Knopf, 1994.

Patterson, Francine, and Eugene Linden. *The Education of Koko*. New York: Holt, Rinehart & Winston, 1981.

Porter, Valerie. *Faithful Companions: The Alliance of Man and Dog*. London: Methuen, 1987.

Searl, Edmund. *In Memoriam: A Guide to Modern Funeral and Memorial Services*. Boston: Skinner House, 1993.

Serpell, James. *In the Company of Animals: A Study of Human-Animal Relationships*. New York: Blackwell, 1986.

Temerlin, Maurice K. *Lucy: Growing Up Human*. Palo Alto, CA: Science and Behavior Books, 1975.

Acknowledgments

ALL THE INCIDENTS recounted in this book are true. In some cases, minor details such as names have been changed to protect confidentiality or to simplify the narrative.

I want to thank the many individuals and organizations who contributed to this work, especially my wife, Dori Jones, who helped with proofreading and offered her usual good advice, but also the following: Liz Frenette of the Monadnock Humane Society; David Walton, PhD; Professor Jeanette Jones of Rutgers University, who besides conducting original research on the emotion of sadness happens to be my sister-in-law; Michael Ward; the International Association of Pet Cemeteries; Mount Auburn Cemetery in Cambridge, Massachusetts;

Patricia Gabel of the Association for Gravestone Studies; Margaret Carter; Professor Robbie Kahn; Holly Cheever, DVM; Holly Busier; Dee Kalea; Gloria Cooley; Errol Sowers, who contributed the story of his dog, Lady; Ann Ashby, who shared her investigations on animal effigies and gravestone inscriptions; Connie Howard of the Greater Burlington Humane Society, who shared her own wisdom and permitted me to photograph animals in the shelter under her care; Iris Muggenthaler of Endtrap; Valerie Hurley and John Kern; and Professor Tom Regan of North Carolina State University. The information and help I received from these and others was invaluable.

I am also indebted to my congregation, the First Unitarian Universalist Society of Burlington, Vermont, for providing me with six months of sabbatical leave, which gave me time to undertake this project. I am grateful as well to the Harvard Divinity School for offering me a Merrill Fellowship in the spring of 1996, thus making it possible for me to use Harvard's libraries and other research facilities.

Finally, my appreciation goes to my publisher, New World Library, for the staff's editorial support and belief in the importance of this subject, enabling me to complete a revised and expanded version of this work. My hope is that those who read this book will find consolation themselves and share this volume with others who are grieving. If it brings a smile or helps to dry a tear, my effort will have been well worthwhile.

Permission Acknowledgments

Grateful acknowledgment is offered to all those who
authorized the use of their work.

About the Author

GARY KOWALSKI began work on *Goodbye, Friend* when his beloved dog Chinook was eleven years old. Chinook died shortly after the publication of the book's first printing and this revised edition is dedicated to his memory.

Since then, Gary has enjoyed the company of another pup named Smokey (part German Shepherd, part kangaroo, and part snapping turtle), as well as a flock of hens named Faith, Hope, Charity, Fred, and Gobbledegook.

A graduate of Harvard College and the Harvard Divinity School, Reverend Kowalski is an ordained minister who has served churches in Tennessee, Washington State, Vermont, New Mexico, and Massachusetts. He is active in the Green Mountain Animal Defenders, an advocacy group working for better treatment of animals in entertainment, research, and agriculture. A committed vegan, he is past president of the Unitarian Universalist Animal Ministry.

Reverend Kowalski is currently working on a new volume titled *Blessings of the Animals* celebrating the variety of creatures, from spring peepers to river otters and migrating geese, who animate our planet.

Visit his website at www.kowalskibooks.com.

NEW WORLD LIBRARY is dedicated to publishing books and other media that inspire and challenge us to improve the quality of our lives and the world.

We are a socially and environmentally aware company, and we strive to embody the ideals presented in our publications. We recognize that we have an ethical responsibility to our customers, our staff members, and our planet.

We serve our customers by creating the finest publications possible on personal growth, creativity, spirituality, wellness, and other areas of emerging importance. We serve New World Library employees with generous benefits, significant profit sharing, and constant encouragement to pursue their most expansive dreams.

As a member of the Green Press Initiative, we print an increasing number of books with soy-based ink on 100 percent postconsumer-waste recycled paper. Also, we power our offices with solar energy and contribute to nonprofit organizations working to make the world a better place for us all.

Our products are available
in bookstores everywhere.
For our catalog, please contact:

New World Library
14 Pamaron Way
Novato, California 94949

Phone: 415-884-2100 or 800-972-6657
Catalog requests: Ext. 50
Orders: Ext. 52
Fax: 415-884-2199
Email: escort@newworldlibrary.com

To subscribe to our electronic newsletter, visit
www.newworldlibrary.com